May God enrich your life through this

HEARING GOD THROUGH PHYSICAL DISORDERS

WHAT'S YOUR BODY SAYING?

FRED C. FROST

iUniverse

HEARING GOD THROUGH PHYSICAL DISORDERS
WHAT'S YOUR BODY SAYING?

Copyright © 2017 Fred C. Frost.

All rights reserved. No part of this book may be used or reproduced by any means, graphic, electronic, or mechanical, including photocopying, recording, taping or by any information storage retrieval system without the written permission of the author except in the case of brief quotations embodied in critical articles and reviews.

The information, ideas, and suggestions in this book are not intended as a substitute for professional medical advice. Before following any suggestions contained in this book, you should consult your personal physician. Neither the author nor the publisher shall be liable or responsible for any loss or damage allegedly arising as a consequence of your use or application of any information or suggestions in this book.

Scripture taken from the King James Version of the Bible. Scripture quotations taken from the Holy Bible, New Living Translation, Copyright © 1996, 2004. Used by permission of Tyndale House Publishers, Inc., Wheaton, Illinois 60189. All rights reserved.

iUniverse books may be ordered through booksellers or by contacting:

iUniverse
1663 Liberty Drive
Bloomington, IN 47403
www.iuniverse.com
1-800-Authors (1-800-288-4677)

Because of the dynamic nature of the Internet, any web addresses or links contained in this book may have changed since publication and may no longer be valid. The views expressed in this work are solely those of the author and do not necessarily reflect the views of the publisher, and the publisher hereby disclaims any responsibility for them.

Any people depicted in stock imagery provided by Thinkstock are models, and such images are being used for illustrative purposes only.
Certain stock imagery © Thinkstock.

ISBN: 978-1-5320-1817-6 (sc)
ISBN: 978-1-5320-1818-3 (e)

Library of Congress Control Number: 2017903958

Print information available on the last page.

iUniverse rev. date: 04/28/2017

In loving memory of my mother, Margaret Lewis Frost.

While on her sickbed, in a state of delirium from the toxins caused by renal failure, my mother inspired and encouraged me to continue to write while I was in a state of procrastination. While in the hospital one night, restless and seemingly confused, she forcefully repeated, "Write it down. Write it down." I got a pen and paper and guided her hand while she scribbled something illegible, but somehow, I knew what it meant. Only after conveying the message to me to complete this book did she fall asleep peacefully that night.

To the memory of my longtime friend and coworker, Dr. Ireneo Domingo.

He had an awesome sense of humor. He told me that he was looking forward to receiving his copy of this book. Maybe God will let him read it in heaven one day.

CONTENTS

Foreword ix
Preface xi
Acknowledgments xv
Introduction xvii

Chapter 1   Why the Blood? 1
Chapter 2   The Spiritual Immune System 11
Chapter 3   Spiritual Germs 26
Chapter 4   Spiritual Wounds 32
Chapter 5   The Purpose of Pain 41
Chapter 6   Spiritual STDs 44
Chapter 7   Spiritual Heart Disease 60
Chapter 8   Spiritual Constipation 70
Chapter 9   Spiritual CPR 77
Chapter 10 Spiritual Hypertension 81
Chapter 11 Spiritual Diabetes 87
Chapter 12 Spiritual Obesity 101
Chapter 13 Spiritual Cancer 104
Chapter 14 Spiritual Lupus 118
Chapter 15 Spiritual Dehydration 122
Chapter 16 Spiritual Pregnancy 128
Chapter 17 Spiritual Transplant Rejection 170
Chapter 18 To Be Continued 173

Resources 175

FOREWORD

Having spent many years at bedsides as an ER nurse, I've seen almost every ailment known to humankind. I've shared in the grief as doctors delivered terrible news and comforted families as loved ones passed on. It has been said that the walls of hospitals have heard more prayers than the walls of a church. It is true that our spiritual being and physical being are closely intertwined; this book highlights that close relationship between our humanity and spirituality.

In this book, Fred Frost takes us on a remarkable journey through human body systems, relating physical ailments and diseases to spiritual ailments and diseases that plague us, a fallen creation. There is much to be learned from these chapters. Fred has taken his many years of nursing experience and vast medical knowledge and created an interesting and informative book that will enable you to see God's hand in everyday afflictions, highlighting the connection between the body and spirit that is found throughout the Bible.

Kim Nelson, DON, MSN, RN

PREFACE

I've worked bivocationally for more than thirty years as a nurse and minister. Although I've heard many people say that a person can't be an effective pastor if he works a secular job, I know in my heart that I was born to do both. I found my niche in the two because I understand nursing to be a ministry and ministry to be nursing and medicine for the soul. It's always very rewarding when I'm able to use what I've learned in the health care field to teach people about spiritual health. This has been my approach for several years, and wherever or whenever I teach from this perspective, I seem to get the strongest response from listeners. I've also discovered that there's never a shortage of sermons while studying the human body, which is why I was compelled to write on this subject of hearing God through physical disorders. Sometimes it may seem as though I'm being a bit generous with the analogies, but people who know me well know that this is the norm for me. And if you follow me closely through these analogies, I believe you will hear God as well.

It started as far back as nursing school, when I initially noticed that I had been given a gift of spiritual insight into the physical body. I could hear God speaking to me through disorders and conditions being taught by my wonderful nursing instructors. I could see God moving and enlightening me through the professors in my biology and anatomy/physiology courses. I've always been very inquisitive by nature, a trait that has helped me learn so much from professional colleagues over the years in the health care field.

I've taken numerous classes with physicians, nurses, paramedics, and others for continuing education credits or certifications. I always find something I can use for ministry when I dig with my spiritual shovel.

I've learned so much in my years of experience while taking care of thousands of patients. I've also learned just as much from wonderful spiritual leaders who have taught me. Caring for people with spiritual needs has been one of my greatest teachers as well. While watching certain diseases and disorders manifest certain symptoms, I would read the Bible and find or diagnose the spiritual condition. It's truly helped me learn from the various conditions we can develop. If you understand that the symptoms a person manifests are the result of a condition or disease, it should cause you to become less judgmental and more sympathetic and empathetic. If the person is acting out of character in any way, you will understand that something is causing the deviant behavior.

There are certain things in this book you may find challenging if you don't have a health care background, but it's not my intention to leave you in the dark. As you would study the Bible, there is some content discussed here that requires more than mere reading—it requires study. This book was birthed from the study of the Bible, the science of the body, and years of clinical experience. The practice of medicine is, in many ways, an art and not an exact science. This is why you'll find varying opinions on the pathology, diagnosis, and treatment of certain diseases. By the time this book is published, some things in medicine will have changed because of new findings from continued research. Just as in medicine, certain basics we learn from the Bible are vital with no grounds for debate; other things we learn through deeper study and research to help us better understand difficult passages and what the Bible originally meant. If you keep this correlation in mind, as I do, you will continually learn fresh insight from the human body as well as the Bible, while learning to hear what your body is saying spiritually.

ACKNOWLEDGMENTS

I would like to acknowledge my Lord and Savior, Jesus Christ, who is the reason I write and minister and for all that I do. The Holy Spirit is my inspiration and enabler who has guided my hand to write while orchestrating this whole work.

Thank you to my family for always being a great support system. My amazing wife, Barbara, has faithfully stood by me over the years while encouraging me to write and complete this book. My siblings also have been of constant support, from childhood to now. My children, Frederick, Desmond, and Kendra, have pushed me, even buying tablets as a gesture to encourage me to stop procrastinating. A special thanks to my daughter, Kendra, who was the editor for this project.

I am definitely grateful for all the awesome physicians, nurses, and health care workers I've worked with and learned from over the years, from Lakeview Community Hospital (currently Medical Center Barbour) in Eufaula, Alabama, to Bullock County Hospital in Union Springs, Alabama. Although health care workers are often underappreciated, they do an incredible job of taking care of people and their health issues. A special thanks to the staff of Bullock County Hospital, who even assisted me with typing.

My wonderful leader, Dr. Ann L. Hardman, founder of the Endowed with Power Ministerial Fellowship, has been a great inspiration to me in the writing of this book. For years I've aspired to complete this book. Connecting with her ministry and seeing her already *doing* inspired me greatly.

A special thanks to all the wonderful people I've been blessed to lead over the years at the New Birth Center of Eufaula, Alabama, and Spirit and Truth of Montgomery, Alabama. You guys are the best! To all my fellow believers and coworkers in ministry, thank you for all the prayers and support over the years.

INTRODUCTION

The human body is such an incredible piece of work that there had to be a divine designer of this remarkable structure. Scriptures confirm this, when David declared in Psalm 139 that he was intricately knitted or woven together by God in his mother's womb and that he was "fearfully and wonderfully made." He says God recorded every detail and moment of our lives in His book while our substance was incomplete and that His thoughts toward us were more in number than the sand. All this suggests that God took great care in the making of these incredible physical specimens. One can't help but notice how true this is when studying the human body. This wasn't just a "let there be" and it was. The Bible says in Genesis 1 and 2 that God created us in His "image" and after His "likeness" when He formed us from the dust of the earth. He put His DNA in us and breathed His life into us, making us uniquely different from the animals. It's amazing to me that chemicals and elements that are found in the soil or earth's crust are the same as those found in our bodies, causing them to function properly. For example, did you know that nearly 75 percent of the earth's surface is covered by water? When we're born, close to 75 percent of our bodies are made up of water.

While on earth, Jesus taught many things by parables, which were earthly stories, illustrations, or analogies to convey spiritual or heavenly truths. In John 3, while teaching Nicodemus about regeneration, Jesus said that he must be "born again." John 3:12 shows us that we first need to understand the natural in order to understand the spiritual things. Even Paul stated in 1 Corinthians

15:44–49 that the natural came first and then the spiritual. He said we have a *natural* or *physical body* and we have a *spiritual body*. Jesus would say things like "blind leaders of the blind" (Matt. 15:14), in which He was comparing spiritual blindness to physical blindness. He was the "bread of life" (John 6:35) for us to consume for spiritual life. Jesus was teaching us to look at our physical bodies to learn what God was saying to us. If things get out of order and the body gets sick or diseased, these are signs to show us how our spiritual lives can get sick and diseased. Over the years, I've learned from connecting my nursing profession with my ministry that every disorder or disease that can happen to us physically can happen to us spiritually. The result for me was a compilation of analogies and insights from the physical body that I've found to be a great asset to believers as well as nonbelievers.

Even in the Old Testament, Deuteronomy 28 teaches us how we're cursed with all types of diseases and physical disorders, such as consumption, fever, burning, blindness, tumors, boils, itching, madness, and all types of problems when we refuse to listen to God. Although these things were spoken to the Israelites under the old covenant, it's all given for our learning as well. And although we may be in Christ, whether actually sinning or not, we still have numerous physical disorders through which God teaches us, if we'll listen. This is why Jesus said those who have ears should listen to what the Spirit is saying to the church. Therefore, it behooves us to listen and learn spiritual messages from the physical body. This is the essence of what this book is about—looking at the physical body to learn from it spiritually.

Paul taught in numerous places, referring to the church as the "body of Christ" (Rom. 12; 1 Cor. 12; Eph. 1). Individually, he says that our bodies are the temple of the Spirit (1 Cor. 3:16–17, 6:19). Collectively, we are the body of Christ, whether in a local church body or community, a denominational or nondenominational fellowship, or universally, the worldwide body of believers. Although Christ's body is perfect, we don't always walk perfectly in Him. When things go awry in our spiritual walk, we should attempt to diagnose it and correct it as soon as possible.

You can see through apostle Paul's teachings that he had great insight into the workings of the human body nearly two thousand years ago. He did it without the convenience of our modern technology. He didn't have access to the Internet to do a Google search. Nor did he have cable or satellite to flip to the Discovery Channel. There was no MRI, CT scan, ultrasound, or any of the great schools of medicine and teaching hospitals to learn about our physical bodies. Therefore, this had to be a revelation from God for Paul to gain insight into the workings and correlation between the physical and spiritual. He talked about the various parts needing each other for the whole body to function properly. He says, "God has set the members, each one of them in the body just as He pleased" (1 Cor. 12:18), and "there should be no schism [division] in the body" (1 Cor. 12:25), because if one suffers, all suffer. The terminology Paul uses in 1 Corinthians 12–14 while discussing the various ministries and spiritual gifts is amazingly similar to our modern terminology. He uses terms like "function," "decently and in order," "division," and so forth. Today, for instance, when evaluating the liver or kidney we hear terms such as "liver function test" or that a person's kidney function is only 20 percent. In cancer, there is an abnormality in cell "division." Therefore, when these systems are not functioning properly (decently and in order), we have "disorders." Could it be that Paul saw "cancer" in the spirit when he said there should be no "division" in the body? Cancer cells are in the body, doing their own thing but causing the whole body to suffer. Perhaps he saw "spiritual lupus," an autoimmune disease in which the body fights against itself.

There are as many disorders and diseases in the spirit as there are diseases and disorders of the physical body. We just have to learn to diagnose and treat these spiritual conditions. They can be just as detrimental to our spiritual bodies as disease is to the physical body. Always bear in mind that physicians even misdiagnose physical conditions at times, so it's okay if we "miss it" sometimes. There are times you may have to get a second opinion. This is also why I say we're "learning" to diagnose spiritual conditions.

We must keep in mind that in order to stay healthy physically and perform at our maximum potential, all our parts must function properly. For instance, if the kidneys simply stop working, the body will die. Remember—we are the church, individually as well as collectively. If you know your gift or calling, and you just don't function, you hurt yourself and the church. James 4:17 says if you know to do good but don't do it, it is sin to you. And the wages of sin is death (Rom. 6:23).

Even if you, as a pastor or leader, don't treat certain conditions, it's helpful to understand what's going on spiritually within your local church body, which enables you to find peace or closure in many instances. Sometimes you may be angry with someone because of the symptoms he or she is manifesting, but if you understood that the person had a certain condition that caused him or her to act that way, you probably would be more sympathetic and empathetic toward that person. The universal body of believers has problems that need to be diagnosed and treated as well. After studying these conditions yourself, you will find that God is speaking to us through them, along with several other conditions that can afflict us. So travel with me through the physical body in this quest to find valuable spiritual truths that can help us in our spiritual journey.

Why the Blood?

Hebrews 9:22 says that without the shedding of blood, there is no remission of sin. First John 1:7 says, "But if we walk in the light as He is in the light, we have fellowship with one another, and the blood of Jesus Christ His Son cleanseth us from all sin."

I'm sure you've pondered the question of why God required the blood sacrifices mentioned in the Bible and, more specifically, why Christ had to shed His blood to cleanse us from our sins. In Genesis 4 we read about the Lord accepting Abel's "blood" sacrifice over his brother Cain's nonchalant "fruit of the ground" offering. When Cain became jealously irate, killing his brother, the Lord said, "The voice of your brother's blood cries out to me from the ground."

Also, Exodus 12 shows us how and where the blood was to be placed on the doorpost—(1) the lintel and (2) the side posts, representing the cross—to protect the children of Israel from the death angel. Thus, seeing the importance of blood throughout scripture, I hope to shed a little light on the subject here.

Leviticus 17:11 states, "For the life of the flesh is in the blood ... to make atonement for your souls." Please note that scripture says "the life of the flesh is in the blood." If this is true, physically, then we know the life of the spiritual man is also in the blood of Christ. Therefore, it behooves us to find out what's in the blood and how it functions within our physical bodies.

As an emergency room nurse for many years, I have noticed that most ER patients are very unnerved, even hysterical, at the sight of their own blood. Educated or not, people don't want to bleed or lose too much blood. They know it can be a matter of life or death.

I've also observed that when a person is truly sick, the physician will order a blood test to see what is in the blood and how much blood the patient has. Vital signs include checking the blood pressure and the pulse, which is felt because of the pressure of blood. When we perform CPR, we're trying to circulate the blood. Blood carries oxygen and nourishment to all the body's tissues and organs and removes waste. If the circulation is cut off for too long, tissues die, organs and systems shut down, and the whole body ultimately dies. During a heart attack, circulation is blocked to the arteries of the heart muscle itself. This could potentially stop the heart from beating and, again, lead to death. You can see the importance of blood and why God told us long ago that the life of the flesh is in the blood.

The blood serves as an awesome transport system within the body. If we understand that we, as believers in the body of Christ, are like the cells making up the physical body, as the blood transports the oxygen and nutrients to our cells for survival, protection, and energy, so does the blood of Christ function for us spiritually. The circulation of blood means that it's constantly on the move, bringing things in as well as removing things from our lives. Therefore, we should always allow the blood to flow freely in our lives and not do anything to impede its flow. Always have a repentant attitude when recognizing something within that could impede the flow of the blood of Jesus in your life.

Within our bodies we have the pulmonary and the systemic

circulation of blood. As you may know, the blood is pumped from the heart through the arteries to all the body's tissues and organs. It returns through the veins to the heart but goes through the pulmonary circulation to exchange gases between the blood and the air. Newly oxygenated blood goes back to the heart; the cycle is constant. The thing to focus on here is the breathing of fresh air to obtain oxygen to circulate through the blood.

The Greek word for "spirit" is *pneuma*, which means wind, air, or breath. John 20:22 says Jesus breathed on His disciples, telling them to receive the Holy Spirit. John 4 tells us that God wants us to worship Him in "spirit" and truth. Just as we have air and blood to live physically, we need the Spirit of God to live spiritually. The Spirit of God flows in our lives through the blood of Christ as oxygen flows through the blood of the human body. This is what Christ is telling us in John 5:53–58; unless we eat His flesh and drink His blood, we have no life in us. In other words, our constant and complete trust in Christ's shed blood and daily walking in the Spirit is the way to eternal life.

Blood Components

The blood contains plasma, the liquid portion, which contains red blood cells, white blood cells, platelets, proteins, and other solutes. Blood, with all its components, is so complex that we'll only discuss a few components in limited detail.

Platelets

The blood has platelets and other blood-clotting factors that keep us from bleeding to death when injured. Just imagine how the blood of Jesus sends clotting elements to our wounds immediately for damage control. As clearly depicted in Isaiah 53, He was wounded for our transgressions, bleeding outwardly for our overt sins but bruised for our iniquities, and bleeding inside for our hidden sins. Here, we can already see elements of His blood saving us. Sometimes all you need is a transfusion of platelets or fresh plasma when the bleeding won't stop. Remember Christ's blood has it all. Trust what He did for you on the cross. Pray, "Lord, I'm hurting. Stop the bleeding," and then He'll cause it to clot. You hold the pressure by not giving up, and He'll make the bleeding stop.

Red Blood Cells

The red blood cells (RBCs), also known as erythrocytes, perform several vital functions. They carry oxygen to the body's cells. Remember that we're individual cells within the church body and require the oxygen brought to us by the blood of Christ. In John 6:63, Christ tells us that the words He speaks are "spirit and life" or oxygen and blood. RBCs also help remove the harmful wasteful product of carbon dioxide by transporting it from the cells (us) to the external environment through the lungs. When the Spirit energizes us through the blood, the waste has to be removed from us. This is where the blood of Christ is working in us to keep us clean while the Spirit is making things happen for us. As you can see, it's vital to have enough RBCs in order to carry the oxygen adequately. If we don't have enough RBCs, we can become anemic, pale, weak, short of breath, and develop other problems, which can lead to death. I'm sure you can already see the correlation spiritually. If we lose too much blood in our spiritual lives, our churches, or ministries, we become anemic, weak, and unable to function properly. Waste builds up in our lives, and we die out spiritually.

Physically, anemia can occur from hemorrhaging. Whether

from bleeding ulcers, internal injuries, or accidents, the bleeding must stop. If you get into an accident or altercation with fellow believers, family members, or even people you don't know and find that you've been injured, get your wounds treated immediately. All types of anemia—such as aplastic, pernicious, and sickle cell—can be dangerous, even deadly, if not treated. Some forms of anemia can occur from exposure to certain toxic chemicals, drugs, viruses, or other conditions. Spiritually, sin and certain things we're exposed to can have a toxic effect on us, causing us to become weak, anemic Christians. Thus, you might have to separate yourself from toxic environments or people.

There's also anemia caused from the lack of "intrinsic factor." This substance allows vitamin B12 to be absorbed from the foods we eat. We have to have enough of this vitamin in the blood to produce the RBCs we need, or we become anemic. Is there a lack of "intrinsic factor" in your belly that's causing you to be spiritually anemic? Is there something within that's causing you to be incapable of absorbing the Word of God? Sometimes you have to do as David did, and ask God to search you, seeing if there's any wicked way within you, and create a clean heart, renewing a right spirit within (Psalms 139 and 51). Initially, David didn't realize the thing within him that was causing his anemia until Nathan, the prophet, confronted him concerning Bathsheba and Uriah. If you repent, God can renew your intrinsic factor. Remember—with any anemia, if your blood count gets too low, you'll need a blood transfusion. This is why Christ donated His blood at the Red Cross on Calvary. There was a cross-match already done. He knows your blood type, and He's the universal donor. Christ came to save us all by shedding His blood on the cross, and it's up to us to keep our blood count up.

White Blood Cells

Now let's take a look at the incredibly fascinating white blood cells (WBCs), or leukocytes. These cells defend the body against cancer cells that form in the body's tissues and protect the body from invading microbes. This concept is so amazing when applied spiritually. Microbes represent sin, evil spirits, and influences of the secular world that are trying to invade our lives and infect us with spiritual diseases. The blood of Christ has the WBCs constantly on guard, ready to defend the body of believers, individually and collectively.

WBC Types and Functions

1. *Neutrophils* are the most numerous circulating WBCs and are active in protecting the body against invading microorganisms. They are called phagocytes because they engulf bacteria, debris, dead tissue cells, and other foreign cells into their cell bodies, digesting it. Isn't this what Christ did for us? While we were dead in sin, trespasses, debris, and foreign particles that consumed our lives, He shed His blood, full of neutrophils to engulf and digest it all to save us. He did ask the Father to let this cup pass but stated, nevertheless, "not my will but thine be done" (Luke 22:42). These WBCs digest the bacteria (sin) and then die a sacrificial death; Christ did the same for us.

    It's awesome to think about what the blood did for us at Calvary, but what amazes me is what the blood is constantly doing for us *now*. Neutrophils are the first-line-of-defense WBCs that are constantly on duty, patrolling throughout the body, looking for bacteria and foreign substances. When certain pathogens invade the body, they emit chemical signals that cause the neutrophils to react and chase them down. Sin too gives off a certain sign that causes the blood of Christ to react. So the blood is ready at all times to chase the invading enemy of sin and evil to destroy it in our lives.

Just as these microbes, or pathogens, that are working to invade our bodies are invisible to the naked eye, sin and unseen forces are constantly at work or opportunistically waiting for an opening to come in and infect us spiritually. This correlation is very vivid and explicit, showing us how we're fighting unseen enemies, both physically and spiritually, but the blood is steadily defending us on both ends as well. This is also seen in Revelation 12, when it says they overcame the devil by the blood of the lamb.

Another interesting point is that when you see pus, it's a good sign that your immune system is doing its job to fight infection. White blood cells in pus are dying that you might live. This sounds familiar, doesn't it? Christ shed His blood that we might live. Sometimes things have to get ugly and stink with pus before they get better, but it's all a part of the process caused by the work of the WBCs. It was ugly and a serious stink that occurred on Calvary when Christ's neutrophils reacted with the spiritual bacteria of sin, causing pus while engulfing the sin.

Even in the death of neutrophils during phagocytosis, they release certain substances that continue to affect the immune system's response, killing bacteria. This is so true with the death of Christ because His death is still working to defeat sin in our lives. The blood is still working to keep us safe.

2. *Eosinophils* have a weak phagocytic effect. They help protect against various parasitic infections. Examples of parasitic infections are toxoplasmosis, lice (head, body,

and pubic), and worms, among others. Parasites get their food and survive off or at the expense of host. They don't always cause disease in the host. People with compromised immune systems are more susceptible. The eosinophils play an important role in defending the body against these types of diseases. Spiritually, parasitic people worm their way into your life, living off you and using you. But Christ's blood protects you from the harm they may cause, if you apply it, for He commanded us to pray for those who spitefully use us, borrowing and not repaying.

Also, eosinophils play an important role in the inflammatory response in the body's immune system. Inflammation is part of the body's response to protect it from germs or other harmful irritants by isolating the foreign substance. There's redness, swelling, pain, and heat at the site of the invasion or injury. And when you think about inflammation, you think about fire, heat, or fever. Thus, the body is getting fired up about an injury or something that shouldn't be there.

We saw Jesus get inflamed when the people were robbing others and turning the temple into something God never intended for it to be. In Matthew 21, Jesus cleansed the temple through the inflammatory response with His indignation. Since the blood is the essence of our lives, it was also what Christ was about. Just as He cleansed the temple in Jerusalem, the blood of Christ cleanses our individual temples and the overall body of Christ. The eosinophils have several functions in this complex immune response, and while some of the functions are not yet understood, it's important to note that they can cause damage to tissue by prolonging inflammation or simply too much inflammation. I would spiritually apply this concept to people who have good intentions in ministry but are too harsh or aggressive at times. The spiritual eosinophils in the blood of Christ, operating under His command, know when to attack and when to back off. I recommend that we all flow in the pulse or heartbeat of God.

3. *Basophils* also play a role in the inflammatory response, along with responding to parasites and ticks. They secrete histamine in the inflammatory response but also produce heparin. Heparin is very potent in keeping the blood from clotting so that it continues to flow where needed. The histamine dilates the vessels so that the blood can flow to the affected area, with the heparin making sure it moves as it should.

    In Isaiah 59, the scriptures declare that "when the enemy comes in like a flood, the Spirit of the Lord will lift up a standard against him." Some Bible teachers say the comma should be placed before the phrase "like a flood," rather than after it. Since the Spirit moves through the blood, it is understood how God's standard is at work against the enemy coming in. The basophils lift up the standard by the histamine and heparin, causing the blood to flood the area, in turn leading to swelling and inflammation. We too should swell at times, rising against the enemy. (We'll go more into detail in the chapter concerning the immune system.)

4. *Monocytes* are similar to neutrophils in their aggressive phagocytic action. They are the largest of the WBCs and can engulf larger germs and even cancerous cells. Some grow into much larger cells, called macrophages. Just as there are larger microbes that these macrophages engulf, eat, or destroy, the blood of Christ deals with the small as well as the greater issues and sins we face.

Some of the macrophages travel through tissues looking for bacteria to engulf, but other macrophages reside in various organs, waiting for invaders. In other words, sin doesn't stand a chance against the blood of Christ, now or later.

5. *Lymphocytes* are white blood cells that protect us from infection in the immune mechanism. There are B lymphocytes and T lymphocytes. The B-cells produce antibodies, which act to destroy certain germs or chemical toxins. The T-cells act directly by attacking specific pathogens or cancerous cells.

This chapter teaches us how the blood of Christ protects us through immunity. Whether directly or indirectly, the blood is constantly at work for us, fighting germs of sin and demonic activity in the kingdom of darkness. As Joseph M. Scriven stated in the old hymn, "O what peace we often forfeit, O what needless pain we bear, all because we do not carry everything to God in prayer." Apply the blood of Christ to every problem you face.

The blood is always moving on our behalf. There's an army of white blood cells and antibodies ready to mobilize at a moment's notice. We always need enough blood and the right amount of blood components to remain healthy, or we'll die. Therefore, we have to make sure we don't do anything to impede the flow. We need the blood in every ministry in order for each to live. Circulate the blood of Christ in your preaching, and the lost will be saved. There's truly wonder-working power in the blood of the lamb!

The Spiritual Immune System

The physical world in which we live is a very dangerous environment, with constant threats to our physical well-being. There's the potential of contracting diseases from parasites, viruses, bacteria, and various toxins in the atmosphere. We even have the threat of cells within our bodies mutating and becoming cancerous. But don't despair. God has installed in us a remarkable defense system. This protective security shield is called the immune system and is always alert and actively defending us against intruders and disease. This system is so complex, with layers of elements and components at work. Since I can only scratch the surface on some of the amazing aspects of it, I encourage you to study and dig deeper, pulling out some of this rich treasure of information and apply it to your life or ministry.

There are numerous pathogens and environmental threats to us physically, and the same is going on against our spiritual bodies. The Bible says that we're wrestling against "spiritual wickedness" and "rulers of darkness" (Eph. 6:12). These unseen forces pose as grave a threat to our spiritual well-being as the things we face physically. Therefore, God has supplied us with an incredible spiritual defense system that guards us against the constant threat of sin and evil spirits in the atmosphere. In one sense, it could be summed up as the grace system of God constantly working on our behalf. When Paul prayed to God three times about a thorn with which a messenger of Satan had attacked him, God told him that His grace would take care of the problem—His strength working through our weakness (see 2 Cor. 12). John 1 also says the law came by Moses and was against us (Rom. 7:7–13), but grace came by Christ. Scripture says Jesus was "full of grace and truth" (John 1:14). Christ brings His immune system to us, and Paul says there is "no condemnation" to us in Him (Rom. 8:1). Ephesians 2 even says we're saved by grace. There are numerous things, such as the armor of God, the blood, angels, and the Spirit of God Himself that work together to keep us from harm. But it's all by His grace toward us.

About the Immune System

The immune system of the human body is more sophisticated than any system that man has ever put together. From the nose, mouth, and eyes, mucus, tears, and saliva are secreted that contain enzymes that destroy bacteria or trap it and remove it. Sweat comes out of the body to prevent germs from going in. These are nonspecific ways that the body defends itself against intruders. Specific defenses are when the body specifically targets certain pathogens to destroy or develops antibodies against certain germs.

Also, it's amazing how tears wash away foreign substances from the eyes and release stress hormones and toxins from the body, but they also contain an enzyme called lysozyme that kills pathogens. The lysozyme in tears attacks bacteria and kills them by breaking down the cell wall. This is verified in scripture when Proverbs 17:22 says, "A merry heart doeth good like a medicine," bringing emotional tears of joy. Another major point is that tears signify repentance, and if we cry out in sorrow to God—for wronging a brother or sister, for example—that repentance destroys the power of spiritual bacteria (sin) in our lives. In other words, it takes away what Satan is using to try to infect us. Grace is always at work for us, but there are times that we have to repent for our wrongs. Jesus said that if we don't forgive people, our Father in heaven won't forgive us. The poison will stay in us. We should always have a repentant heart, as He told us in the Lord's Prayer: "Forgive us our debts as we forgive our debtors" (Matt. 6:12).

The body reacts to defend itself when exposed to antigens. There's either an inflammatory response locally or a systemic response. When we get fevers, it's a systemic response to get rid of something foreign. The body turns the temperature up to kill off pathogens. The fever makes us feel bad, but it's actually trying to help us. Sin is an antigen that causes an inflammatory response in a healthy individual. If you or your church never gets angry or heated over sin (spiritual fever), maybe it's because your spiritual immune system has been compromised. You should feel sick when sin is in your life or in your church fellowship. On the other hand, if your fever is too high for too long, you can become dehydrated, delirious, or even have seizures and die. In other words, if you stay upset over sin too long or get too angry about it, it can be harmful to your spiritual well-being. Your fever or anger is just a sign that you need to do something to treat the cause of it.

Physically, our bodies have many defense mechanisms in place to protect us. When we eat, there's acid in the stomach that kills many germs from the things we eat or drink. Sneezing, runny noses, watery eyes, coughing up mucus, swelling, fever, and so many more responses are just some of the ways the body defends itself against foreign substances. You can see the tears and mucus, but the microscopic T-cells, B-cells, and antibodies at work are doing their job covertly just as well through humoral and cell-mediated responses. Spiritually, being in Christ, His body has all the defense mechanisms in place to safeguard our souls. It's working even when we're not aware of it, keeping us through dangers, seen and unseen.

Problems Occurring with the Immune System

HIV/AIDS is considered an STD that is caused by having unprotected sex or sharing contaminated needles with drug use. Mothers can pass it on to their children. Certain cells that fight infection are destroyed by the virus and result in a slow destruction of the immune system (see chapter 6 "Spiritual STDs"). The "bubble boy disease" is another immunodeficiency condition (SCID) that causes the body to be unable to fight infection. Autoimmune disorders such as lupus (see chapter 14, "Spiritual Lupus") and rheumatoid arthritis are examples of the immune system attacking its own tissue as something foreign.

Allergic disorders, such as allergies, asthma, and eczema, are examples of conditions where the body overreacts to a foreign substance. Most of the time these substances are relatively harmless. This is an important spiritual message as well. We should react with an inflammatory response if the foreign substance is sin or the devil, but to be hypersensitive to a certain thing that we should be able to handle with ease is a spiritual allergy. It's when people do certain things that are generally harmless, but those things upset you and cause you to be judgmental or unduly critical of them because they aren't doing what you think they should do. It's impossible to live in this world without being exposed to things that are against our moral values, but we shouldn't let it get under our skin (hives, itching). Also, I think many parents have spiritual allergies over relatively harmless things their children do or get involved with because they "didn't teach them that way." Our children are part of us, and we think we're protecting them when we could, in fact, be harming them as well as ourselves with this hypersensitivity or overly defensive immune response. We could be driving them away with our overactive system of moral values. Get into the Word of God and find a dose of spiritual allergy medicine. Take a dose of the "peace of God," and allow it to rule in your heart. Bring it down a thousand!

Anaphylactic shock is an extreme case of overreaction to an antigen. This is when the hypersensitivity can lead to swelling, irregular heart rhythms, and airway constriction, which is life-threatening. An example of this happening spiritually is when someone you least expect does something wrong in the church or in your home that shocks or upsets you so badly that you don't go back to church anymore. For example. if the pastor sins or his daughter becomes pregnant outside of wedlock, you may get upset because you didn't think he or she would do that; this could be dangerous to you, especially after you've listened to his teaching. You may say, "I'll never go to church again because of all of those hypocrites there." You had a spiritually life-threatening experience and if not treated rapidly, it could take you out. Get with your spiritual leader or someone who can give you a shot of spiritual epinephrine (adrenaline) before your life spirals out of control.

Some Components of the Immune System

The skin is the first line of defense against germs. It covers the entire body like a giant sensory, antimicrobial body wrap. It's a protective barrier for our insides against a harsh outside world. It produces sweat and secretes oil and certain substances that fight against intruders. Though we have germs all over our bodies constantly, the skin is generally impenetrable to microbes. As believers, God has anointed us with the oil of His Spirit to protect our treasure that we house in earthen vessels. Sin and evil spirits can't penetrate our anointing or clothing of power unless we allow it to. Sin, as in Genesis 4, is crouching at the door, just as opportunistic germs are waiting for a break in our skin or breach in our security system. They both are waiting to invade and infect us physically and spiritually. Even if there's a breach, the alarm is sounded and repairs and other antimicrobial defenses are initiated immediately. The Bible says God doesn't want us to sin, but if we do, we have an advocate, Jesus Christ, who's constantly making intercession for us. This is why He instructed us to pray like this: "Lead us not into temptation but deliver us from evil" (Matt. 6:13).

The lymphatic system works very closely with the immune system and houses many of its vital components. There are various organs, vessels, tissues, and cells of this system, including the thymus, tonsils, spleen, lymph nodes, lymphocytes, antibodies, and others. It's often referred to as the "drainage" system of the body. The plasma that's pushed out of the bloodstream washes over tissues, carrying bacteria and debris through the lymphatic system, where it's called lymph. It's filtered through the lymph nodes and cleansed and then carried back to the blood. As you can see, this drainage system is very vital to keeping us clean, but it also works closely with the blood. Our spiritual immune system of grace works closely with the blood of Christ. The grace filters our lives of sin, and the blood of Christ removes the waste of it from us. The scriptures confirm this as well, in 1 John 1:7, saying that the blood of Christ "cleanseth us from all sin."

Lymph nodes are filters located in clusters throughout our bodies, all along the pathway of the lymphatic vessels. They defend the body against intruders like bacteria and cancer cells by filtering them out, as well as producing white blood cells. They keep the local infections from entering the blood and spreading to other parts of the body. Sometimes you may notice tenderness under your arm, in your groin, or in your neck area when you have a sore or bump in the area; the area is locally inflamed and trying to make sure that it goes no further. These lymph nodes sound like good old-fashioned intercessory prayer warriors who are lined throughout the body of Christ, defending against invasions of sin, evil spirits, and spiritual cancer cells of false prophets, teachers, or twisted Christians. They get inflamed, on fire spiritually, and prayerfully warn the young men and women to beware of certain predators lurking in the area who mean them no good. We definitely need these spiritual lymph nodes in our lives, ministries, and churches, filtering out and stopping the works of darkness in its tracks.

Tonsils and adenoids are masses of lymphoid tissue located in the mouth, back of the throat, and nasal cavity. When I was a child, I used to hear quite frequently about other children getting tonsils removed without much thought, but in recent years, we've realized that they are there for a reason. Guidelines have changed, and it's recommended to remove tonsils only if a child has recurrent throat infections or breathing problems. Some findings suggest that tonsils are more important during the first few years of life. Tonsils are placed strategically near the entrance of the nose and throat to help defend the body against germs. This is where we eat, drink, and breathe. We definitely need to prayerfully guard against what comes into our spirits. Since we can't protect ourselves against all the things to which we are exposed, we need to rely on the things God already has in place to help us.

The blood is so vital to our survival (see chapter 1, "Why the Blood?") and works closely with the immune system. Certain immune cells are constantly circulating through the blood, patrolling to protect us against foreign invaders. We can't overemphasize the importance of the blood in defending us against sin and evil spirits. The Bible says that God's people overcame Satan by the "blood of the lamb" (Rev. 12). Exodus 12 says that the children of Israel were protected from the death plague by the "blood." Therefore, we must always be vigilant to apply and circulate what Christ did for us on the cross in order to stay covered.

I could discuss numerous other things—bone marrow (where most defense cells are produced), lymphatic tissue in the bowel and certain mucus membranes (over half the cells that produce antibodies are in the gut), spleen (which stores different defense cells that are released when needed), thymus (where certain cells are differentiated or mature)—but this subject is too vast to do it justice here. Everything is placed strategically by God throughout the body for a reason, and each can be applied with a potent spiritual message. From here on, I'll mention only some of the points that grabbed my attention, primarily through definitions and spiritual applications.

Types of Immunity and Functioning of the Immune System

We're born with nonspecific immunity; it's often referred to as innate immunity. This causes the body to attack anything abnormal that threatens its well-being. There should be a readiness to spiritually defend ourselves—or the body of Christ, in general—against anything that threatens our spiritual well-being.

Specific immunity is also referred to as adaptive immunity because of its ability to adapt to new and very specific protection against certain types of germs and toxins. This involves memory and recognition of certain foreign substances. We should have enough of the Word and values instilled in us that certain things automatically trigger a defense against harmful things that enter our lives.

Inflammatory response, as mentioned earlier, is an example of a nonspecific immune response that happens when substances, like bacteria, enter the body, causing tissue damage. Inflammatory response actually is a set of responses that triggers a release from different immune cells. They may contain or destroy bacteria. There's heat, swelling, and pain caused by increased blood flow. At the heart of our spiritual defense is an increase in "blood flow." The pain caused by this response should be a reminder of the pain and blood flow caused by sin at Calvary. Sin should cause us to get hot and swollen against it. There should be a cry that causes a chain reaction of prayer and intercession to contain the sin and start the repair. The grace of God not only defends us, but it also repairs us.

Antibodies are produced by B-cells (also called B-lymphocytes) in response to certain antigens that invade the body. Antigens are substances found on the surfaces of germs or cancer cells. Antibodies are the protective good guys in the body that fight off the invading bad guys called antigens. Antibodies are activated specifically to bind to certain antigens to make them harmless to the body, working like a lock-and-key system. It's like what Jesus said in Matthew 16:19 and 18:18, declaring that He would give us the *keys* of the kingdom of heaven in order to bind whatever was unlawful on earth. Just as antigens are unlawful or not permitted in the physical body by the immune system, sin is not permitted in the body of Christ or the kingdom of God. It must be dealt with as rapidly as the immune system deals with germs to prevent further damage and the spreading of infection.

Antibodies work through the blood and body fluids (humoral immunity), binding, inactivating, or promoting destruction of invading cells. Antibodies also work through a process called complement cascade. During this process, antigens change the antibodies, causing exposure of certain hidden areas of the molecule. When this occurs, certain inactive proteins in the blood called complement come alive and specifically target certain invading cells for destruction. This rapid-fire process is a series of events that results in the destruction of the foreign cells by literally boring holes into them. Sodium enters, allowing water to come in and burst the cells open. When sin invades the church, our homes, or our communities, it often activates people that you didn't know cared at all. God has complementing people who will start a rapid-fire prayer chain to help us in times of need to fight sin and foreign spiritual invaders. The salt of the earth, or believers (see Matt. 5:13), moving among us like the sodium does, will cause the water of the Spirit to come in like a flood against our enemies. It's truly a blessing to have fellow believers who will cause you to be convicted of sin just by their being around you as salt, which conducts electricity. They love you enough to hold you accountable if you get off course.

Lymphocytes are the most numerous types of cells of the immune system and primarily fight infection through memory and producing antibodies. Lymphocytes are located throughout the body, constantly circulating and patrolling through the body's fluids in search of foreign invaders (also see chapter 1, "Why the Blood?"). They're in lymph tissue, lymph nodes, the thymus gland, spleen, and liver. We are greatly covered with a mighty defense system. The primary types of lymphocytes are the B-cells (B-lymphocytes) and the T-cells (T-lymphocytes). It amazes me that lymphocytes originate in the bone marrow because Hebrews 4:12 speaks of the Word of God being alive and going all the way down to the bone marrow. His Word will boost our immune system from the very core of our beings.

The B-cells are like the intelligence system of the military that collects information and is always prepared for war. These cells deal more with memory. When exposed to an antigen, these cells remember the encounter and take note so that when the next encounter happens, they will know to release antibodies for the attack. We should gather as much information on our enemy and his tactics as possible, as well as the deadly effects of sin. After we're exposed to sin and its sickening effect, we should be ready the next time to fight it off. Our consciences should have memory cells stored up, ready to secrete antibodies, which cause us to resist the temptation to sin or succumb to it. This is why the scriptures instruct us to "let" the mind that was in Christ be in us (Phil. 2:5). Also, Psalm 119:11 speaks about hiding God's Word in our hearts so that we won't sin against Him. Never forget how bad sin is, and always be on alert, asking God for help. Also, Jesus said the Holy Spirit would bring the Word that we've been taught back to our memories (John 14:26).

The T-cells initially mature in the thymus and are released into the blood and mainly move to live in the lymph nodes. They contain molecules that are made to fit only one type of antigen. This is why I believe God gives each of us a unique testimony in order to reach a certain type of individual. You are made to bind to a certain individual or type of individual in a specific sin in order to reach them. You've gone through your tests for a reason. You may have even failed some of them, but don't let it be for naught.

The next stage of T-cell development occurs when they encounter an antigen, which causes them to be sensitized. Some of these cells directly kill certain invading cells. Other T-cells do it indirectly by releasing certain substances that attract macrophages, which engulf and destroy the invaders. Things arise in your life that you should attack and destroy directly by being straightforward. Other times, however, a prayerful cry released from your spirit to God or a fellow believer who can come and digest it for you through intercession is the way to get it done.

Sin should sensitize you to act against it. Your prayer cells release a deadly effect against sin. This is what James 5:16 says when he declares that fervent prayers of righteous people have great potential. Remember—we're only righteous through Christ, and we must rely on His immune system (grace) working through us.

Natural and Artificial Immunity

It can be somewhat challenging to fully grasp the different types of immunity, especially when looking at the specific (adaptive immunity) and nonspecific (innate immunity) and the further breakdown of specific immunity into natural and artificial immunity. On top of this, there are the ways the latter two are acquired and considered "active" or "passive" immunity. But the message here is powerful and worth the study.

It's not "if" our physical bodies will be attacked but "when." During specific immunity, the first attack by a particular germ causes symptoms of disease because the body is fighting to destroy the invader. But the next encounter may not cause serious symptoms because the body's immune system recognizes and destroys the pathogen quite rapidly. The person is then said to be immune to that pathogen or organism. Just because a person is immune to one infectious disease doesn't mean that he or she is immune to others. In this spiritual walk, we're constantly exposed to different types of evil spirits and sinful influences; certain things may catch us off guard the first time but subsequent exposure is harmless because we have acquired a spiritual immunity. We have learned better so we can deal with that problem more effectively.

Natural immunity occurs when our exposure to certain germs is not deliberate. An example of this is when a child has active exposure to the measles virus and gets the measles. We should be living our Christian lives by growing in grace and knowledge, with resulting spiritual immunity daily. We should learn from our mistakes as we age, while gaining valuable life experience. The same things shouldn't repeatedly knock us down.

Passive immunity occurs when a mother has had a disease and develops antibodies and then passes them to her unborn child or through her milk when nursing. This is a temporary immunity but protects the child right away. This is why it's so vital to have a spiritual covering from a caring, nurturing leader early in your spiritual walk. Moses covered Joshua, and Elijah covered Elisha. Ephesians 6 says children should "obey your parents in the Lord" and honor parents so that it may be "well" with thee. Spiritual leaders are to pass on the immunity they've acquired to their spiritual children.

Artificial immunity is a deliberate exposure to a potentially harmful pathogen and is also known as immunization. This could be from active exposure, as when children get the polio vaccine, or passive exposure, when injected with antibodies developed by another person's immune system. We need protection against very dangerous and contagious diseases, such as smallpox, polio, and measles. Many vaccines are made from killed or weakened forms of these microbes, which cause the body's immune system to react, destroy, and remember it for the next exposure. Antibodies are developed, and they react and cause destruction of the germs when exposed to it again.

In church or in our homes, we should vaccinate our children with good teachings. Expose them to weakened or harmless versions of the sin at church. Share your bad experiences with your children or the effects of those sins on others who may have developed immunity to certain things that are deadly, such as drugs and alcohol. There are people who have taken kids to correctional facilities and scared them or attempted to "scare them straight." My wife and I taught our young children about the deadly effects of cigarette smoking. Later, my wife took them to a store, and when they saw a man smoking, they yelled to him, "Ooo, you gonna die." The man's eyes widened in amazement. He said, "Okay," and stepped on his cigarette. We all laughed, but their immune systems had kicked in to fight off what they had been vaccinated against at home. This is what Moses instructed the children of Israel to do before entering Canaan, as described in Deuteronomy 6. They were to love God and teach their children His commandments and statutes. Deuteronomy 7 taught them to be careful of the people of that land who could turn their children to other gods. He was, in essence, building up their immune systems before their exposure to the contagious influences of sin that had infected those people. In Deuteronomy 8, God let them know that He led them through this path in the wilderness for forty years for a reason. He deliberately exposed them to certain things so that they might develop immunity to certain things through their experience. In this case, He humbled them so they would always remember that it was He who was their provider.

Christ: Our Ultimate Immunity

As you have seen, there are several types of immunity and means of acquiring them. There are things that protect you merely by being in a good, healthy spiritual environment. Sometimes it's the teachings instilled in you that come back to your memory to guard you. At other times, you learn the hard way, through your mistakes, incidental exposure, and falling into sin. But the ultimate immunity comes from our Lord and Savior Jesus Christ. He deliberately exposed Himself to sin, becoming vulnerable to Satan, sin, and death, in order to create immunity for us. The antibodies were developed in His body when He "who knew no sin" became sin for us (2 Cor. 5:21). He passed on a passive immunity to us through our spiritual rebirth. Just as we get immediate protection from our mothers, physically, so do we get immediate protection from Christ's shed blood when we're born again. The other aspect of this is that passive immunity from mothers is temporary, and active immunity generally lasts longer than the passive immunity. I would say only that you should continue to trust in what Christ did for you but also understand that you have a part to play in this as well. Make it your business to continue to grow in grace. James 4 says that God gives us more grace if we humble ourselves, and only then can we resist the devil. This is also evident in Romans 6, when Paul says sin shall not reign or have dominion in our bodies. Understand that where there's much sin at work, there's much more grace to help. The vaccine against sin is available, but you must keep your immunization up to date.

We have so much in place that is working for our good, according to the scriptures. Even when people or the devil means to hurt us, God works it for our good while bolstering our immune system (Gen. 50:20). God has angels watching over us (Ps. 91:11). When we unify and pray, heaven is watching and has our backs. Romans 8 says we're "more than conquerors" through Christ. Isaiah 54:17 declares, "No weapon that's formed against us" will work. Psalm 125 says that if we trust God, we'll "be like Mount Zion, which cannot be removed but abideth forever." We will have eternal spiritual immunity.

Spiritual Germs

Before really going into diseases and disorders, let's look at some of their major causes by exploring the small yet fascinating world of microbes and parasites. While invisible to the naked eye, they cause so many diseases, infections, disorders, and illnesses. Certain germs thrive in particular environments. You already may see a major parallel with their spiritual counterparts.

Microbes, also known as germs, have been around for as long as the human race has been here. Microbiologist say there are said to be millions upon millions of bacteria all over our bodies, even within. What does this sound like? Sin, perhaps? We are born in sin and shaped in iniquity, says David in Psalm 51. We have all types of sinful desires lurking within us. Like bacteria, sin is in the air, on the ground, and all around us, and it comes in all shapes and forms. Some germs, like Ebola and anthrax, are so deadly that we must carefully guard ourselves against them. Germs such as those that cause tuberculosis can hide in the body for years while evading certain powerful antibiotics and later infect you all over again.

Ephesians 6 speaks of a constant spiritual war going on with unseen spirits and forces. This sounds like parasites and viruses to me. Viruses need a living host to replicate and cause disease.

Demonic spirits require living hosts. If you allow an evil spirit to come inside you, it will use your body to do sinful and harmful things to you and to others. Consider the legion that tormented the man and had him cutting himself. The demons asked Jesus if they could enter the swine (Mark 5; Luke 8). Sometimes we're not possessed by the evil spirits but are oppressed or temporarily infected by them. Scriptures tell us that Jesus cast out and healed many who were oppressed by the devil. Evil spirits are spiritual viruses and parasites that are looking for someone to be their host.

Parasites may cause aggravating conditions or even result in self-limiting symptoms, such as diarrhea. As a whole, they don't want to kill their host because they are using its resources for survival as well. Spiritually, there are evil systems, principalities, or oppressive governments in place that take advantage of people, which could include various racially charged supremacy groups or governments that approve of slave labor to build their empires. They use the people to get rich or use just enough to keep their systems working. Individual people can have parasitic spirits, where those spirits "worm" their way into their lives and live off them and their resources. A person who refuses to work and only wants to live off the government often acts as a parasite. Any individual or system that lives off others may be a parasitic spirit.

There are fungal infections that are hard to treat. You may get ringworm or another fungal infection from rubbing against someone or something dirty. Hanging around certain places or people, breathing unclean air, can often lead to a fungal infection in the lungs that's difficult to treat, especially if the immune system is suppressed. At times, you may go to certain places like strip clubs or nightclubs and then say, "I just hang out there. I don't bother anyone," but you still may get infected. This becomes evident when you develop thoughts, feelings, or imaginings that you can't shake, which can lead to deeper problems. My friend, the world of germs is very real and can be extremely dangerous. Just as your physical body can be infected with these unseen creatures, so can the spiritual body contract all types of infections, diseases, and spiritual disorders that result in a sin-sick soul. As the line can be blurred between bacteria and viruses, as they share many of the same symptoms, so can it blur between sin and demonic possession or oppression. Sometimes in scripture, sin is personified, as in Genesis 4, when God told Cain that if he didn't do well, sin was lying at the door, and "its desire is for you."

How do we deal with this unseen world of enemies that we're wrestling against? In Ephesians 2, we find Satan described as a great evil ruler over the air or atmosphere. Paul told us what to do in Ephesians 6—put on the whole armor of God, always being alert. This is the same thing we're told in the health care profession, which is to use universal precautions. Take coughing, for instance; any time someone coughs around us, we automatically try to shield ourselves from whatever sickness may have produced the cough and is contagious. Coughing is a symptom that could be caused by a cold virus, as well as by the flu, pneumonia, or tuberculosis, just to name a few. Spiritually, a person could be coughing up gossip or negative talk. So if you find yourself gossiping, complaining, or expressing the same symptoms as someone else, you could've been infected through association. This is why it's so important to always be on the watch and use universal precautions—anyone, no matter how the person looks or seems, could be infected by an unseen spirit, disease, or condition that could be contagious. Stay covered under the blood of Christ, always keeping your hands clean with regular repentance. You may have to go the spiritual ER, the altar, if you can't shake the symptoms. Get prayer to serve as a shot of antibiotics; get a scripture from your pastor to serve as your prescription. You may have to rest and drink plenty of fluids. Sounds like a sabbatical with God. Seven days, ten days, twenty-one days, and so forth—pray once or even four times daily about that problem until it clears up.

There's no cure for some of the infections or diseases that you may contract in the natural, but Christ is the cure for every sin-sick soul. He's immune to sin. We need His immune system to keep us, even after we're saved. Isaiah 53:5 speaks of Christ's being wounded for our transgressions and bruised for our iniquities so that we can be healed. As Christ was wounded outwardly for our transgressions that are outwardly obvious to all, He bled inwardly for all our inner iniquities—wrongs that are not so obvious to others. There is still power in the blood. Let Christ live His life through you. Trust in the finished work of Christ on the cross.

Physicians often have difficulty diagnosing conditions. They do differential diagnosis, which is a process of listing all conditions that could possibly be causing the symptoms you exhibit. Blood tests or x-rays may be ordered to find the true diagnosis. Even with an experienced, knowledgeable physician, with access to staff and technicians to run tests and assist with the process, patients still may be misdiagnosed. Understanding this, we definitely would not want to make a practice of treating ourselves physically or spiritually. Just as there are natural physicians, radiologists, ultrasonographers, and nuclear medicine workers who are seers through technology, God has spiritual physicians—pastors, "seers," prophets, and preachers—with spiritual gifts to help see and diagnose spiritual conditions.

Bacterial, viral, and fungal infections can easily get out of control. Therefore, the sooner you get diagnosed and treated, the better. Chapter 6, "Spiritual STDs," explains how the AIDS virus works by attacking the immune system. As a result, AIDS patients often contract opportunistic infections. Germs that a healthy body or immune system would be able to handle, fight off, or keep at bay infect the immunocompromised person.

Germs can enter our bodies through a number of ways: eyes, mouths, ears, noses, genitals, or rectum. There's also the possibility of entering through skin breakage. Here, I'll focus momentarily on wounds or cuts because we could go on endlessly discussing parasites, worms, and flies burrowing through intact skin. Even insect or animal bites can cause major infections. There are times when we may become injured through an accident or someone intentionally cutting us. Either way, we have a wound that needs to be treated because of the break in the skin. Germs, which can never be totally sterilized, are already in countless numbers on our skin and ready to invade, causing infection. Even though the skin is our first line of defense, we must take care of it by attempting to keep out germs to prevent infection. Relating this spiritually, no matter the cause of our wounds or hurts, whether we have accidentally injured ourselves or someone else was to blame, we still have wounds that need to be treated in order to prevent infection spiritually. If left untreated, infection can set in, spread, and cause a loss of limb or life. If the infection gets into the bloodstream, we could become septic and die. The same thing was declared by James when he said, "When lust hath conceived it brings forth sin, when sin is finished it brings forth death" (James 1:15). If you're cut physically, the wound may be irrigated with saline, closed, and then covered. Water is often symbolic of the Spirit in scripture. Therefore, let Christ irrigate your wound with His Spirit, close it to start the healing process, and keep it "covered"—in prayer. Don't put your dirty hands in it or let someone else contaminate your wound. Don't let others cause you to keep digging into it yourself either.

Using universal precautions in health care to protect ourselves against these tiny, deadly pathogens is comparable to putting on the whole armor of God to combat the unseen forces in the spiritual realm. In the health care setting, we have gloves, gowns, masks, goggles, face shields, and shoe covers. The Bible warns us to always be sober, alert, or vigilant because the devil is always on the prowl, seeking to devour us. Never take anyone for granted by assuming he or she is not infected. Anyone at any time, no matter how beautiful or handsome, could pass something on to you if you don't use your spiritual universal precautions.

Trust God, living by faith. Keep your hands clean, and don't go by what you see.

Spiritual Wounds

There's such a plethora of different types of wounds, causes, and treatments that we'll have to seriously limit our discussion here. Some elements of this discussion are related to the chapters on microbes and pain because wounds hurt and have to be kept clean to avoid infection.

Wounds can occur from accidents, causing trauma, or they can be self-inflicted. They can come from burns, bites, stabbings, surgery, gunshots, infections, frostbite, poor circulation, or pressure sores. No matter the cause, wounds need to be treated. Injury is a general term referring to damage to the body, but wounds are generally injuries that break the skin or other tissues within the body.

Millions of people are injured yearly and have wounds that require treatment. With this fact in mind, we have to know that the spiritual implication from this is enormous. We get wounds from the fiery darts of the wicked (Eph. 6:16). Sometimes we're careless and injure ourselves. We may be in a fiery trial of life and get "burned." Jesus said that if our hand or foot causes us to sin, "cut it off" (Mark 9:43–45). In doing so, this will leave a wound that needs to be treated. With Christ being our Great Physician, in John 15, Jesus speaks of pruning us, doing surgery on us to remove certain things from our lives. Even the Word of God is described as being sharper than any two-edged sword, and often, the minister wields it, cutting things from us and at times cutting us unintentionally. Either way, there are wounds that need to be treated. Things to consider when examining a wound are its depth—some are deeper than others—and its location; if a wound is near a vital organ, it can result in a debilitating injury or possibly death.

As stated, we'll only scratch the surface of this subject as I touch on a few points. I encourage you to do your own studies on this because many treatments are based on the circumstances and mechanism of the injury as well as the medical history of the person involved. No matter how cautious we are, most of us will sustain a wound at some time in our lives, but prevention is always the best treatment. Accidents often occur when tools aren't used appropriately. If we don't "rightly divide the word of truth," we could unintentionally injure others or ourselves (2 Tim. 2:15). If we're in a rush or trying to take a shortcut, injuries can occur. Sometimes we're so impatient or ambitious in ministry, desiring to succeed, we have accidents.

Another point is that we should always wear appropriate protective gear. If, while working in the physical world, we have to put on our goggles, helmets, boots, or gloves to protect our bodies, how much more should we guard our spiritual bodies? We do this by dressing in the whole armor of God while working in the kingdom (Eph. 6).

Some minor wounds can be cleaned and dressed at home. In other words, we don't always have to go to the pastor or church with every scrape or ding in our spiritual lives. If you have a cut that's open and bleeding, you'll want to apply pressure to stop the bleeding. Spiritually, if someone is wounded, don't just try to fix it right away, giving away all your answers and scriptures just to stop the bleeding. Apply pressure, a hug, just letting the person know you care and are there for him or her. If the wound needs to be stitched (sutured) or stapled, you may need to get professional help. Your minister or Christian counselor may be the one to help get that wound closed.

If people don't know what they're doing, they could get your wound infected or leave you with an ugly scar. For multiple or deeper wounds, physically, you may have to get transferred to a trauma center. There are burn centers and wound-care clinics. For example, some ministries specialize in assisting hurting, battered women. Sometimes you have to face the fact that your church or ministry may not have what it takes to properly address certain issues people have. I'm sure you've heard of egotistical physicians who try to play God, letting people suffer unnecessarily because they're too proud to refer their patients to another physician. You may not be the one to help them.

A wound or laceration that needs suturing can't be left open too long because it causes a greater risk of infection. Some sources say the wound should be closed within six to twelve hours. I think this is saying if you're angry, hurt, or offended or wounded, don't let the sun go down on your wrath (Eph. 4:26). The longer you stay angry, or with an open wound, the greater the risk of spiritual infection. If the wound is too old or too dirty, it may *have* to be left open to heal from the inside out. The wound is still covered but not closed after cleansing. Allow God's Spirit to irrigate your wound, repenting, getting all the dirt or foreign material from it. Keep it covered with a sterile dressing of love, the antibiotic ointment of prayer, and the Word.

Sometimes, spiritually we don't even realize we have been wounded. But as the skin's initial response to injury is inflammation, spiritually or emotionally, if you become angry, hot, or "inflamed," you've probably been wounded. At this point, you have to determine the type of wound. Animal or human bites are at high risk of getting infected. The main objective of wound care is to promote healing and prevent infection while minimizing scarring. The infection could spread and cause the loss of a limb or your life. If you find yourself getting really sick, are always upset, and can't shake off what someone did to you, the wound may already be infected, and the infection has spread. You may need to seek immediate spiritual help before it destroys you.

Animal Bites

I spoke of animal and human bites, both with a high risk of getting infected. Knowing that there are millions of species of animals, I can only speak in general here. But when we read scripture, we see God comparing things from the natural to the spiritual in numerous passages. He also compares people, Satan, and evil spirits to animals throughout the Bible. For example, you see Satan as a serpent, a dragon, "as a roaring lion," or a wolf out to devour the sheep. He speaks of certain religious leaders as vipers. And certainly in the symbolism of Revelation, He speaks of a beast like a leopard, bear, and lion, which was given power by the dragon. And let's not forget that Jesus gives us power to tread on serpents and scorpions (Luke 19; Mark 16). He tells us in Ephesians 6:12 that we're not wrestling against flesh and blood but huge numbers of wicked spirits in the unseen world. Understanding how these various animals bite or injure their prey or adversaries should give us some insight into the type of wounds we can get spiritually. If a rabid animal bites you, whether a fox, wolf, dog, raccoon, or bat, you know that you not only have the potential for a local infection but also death from a generalized or systemic infection like rabies. It seemed like Job was attacked by Satan out of the blue. He was seriously wounded in this assault on his family, finances, friends, and health, but God delivered and healed him through his steadfast faith.

Look at the children of Israel in the wilderness when they were bitten by the serpents (see Numbers 21). God told Moses to erect the bronze serpent and instructed the people to look, telling them they would live if they had been bitten. They had already been bitten and poisoned spiritually, causing them to sin, speaking against Moses and God. They were discouraged, hurt, angry, and wounded and began to complain. Satan takes advantage of us in our vulnerability, but just because we've been bitten, we don't have to die. Jesus compared Himself to this bronze serpent in John 3:14–15, saying that as Moses lifted up the serpent in the wilderness, even so must the Son of Man be lifted up to give us eternal life if we believe. As the serpent on the pole heals, Christ on the cross heals. Amazingly, venom from the serpent is used to make the antivenin for the poisoning of a snake bite. Second Corinthians 5:21 says Christ was made to be sin for us, who knew no sin, "that we might become the righteousness of God in Him." He became our antivenin. Galatians 3:13–14 tells us that Christ was made a curse for us, being hung on a tree so that the blessing of Abraham might come upon us. Another passage states Christ was "wounded for our transgressions, bruised for our iniquities; ... and with His stripes we are healed" (Isa. 53:5). All His wounds and bleeding were to save and heal us, all through death on the cross.

When bitten by an animal, you may have to get a tetanus vaccine or rabies shots. These vaccines, as well as many others, are made from the germs themselves but have been rendered harmless. Then they're injected into the body so that the body develops antibodies to fight against infectious, potentially deadly diseases. Although we discuss immunity in more detail in chapters on the blood and the immune system, I want to mention how

Jesus took sin into His body for us to render it harmless so we could fight this infectious disease of sin and receive immunity. Knowing that we all get injured from time to time, it's always better if we are up to date on our vaccines. In Genesis, it tells us if we don't do well, sin is at the door. Just as germs are all over our bodies trying to get in, waiting for cuts or openings in our first line of defense (the skin), sin, Satan, and his demons are always opportunistically waiting at the door to come in and hurt, infect, cripple, or scar us. But as Christ used His wounds on the cross to save and heal us, we must take up our crosses, using our wounds to heal and save others.

Human Bites

According to the Mayo Clinic, the human bite, in many cases, is potentially more dangerous than many animal bites because of all the germs in the human mouth. They can transmit germs, causing local infections or even systemic diseases. As we apply this spiritually, we must remember that the animals represent the different types of spirits in the spiritual realm (Eph. 6). Animals just do what animals do instinctively. Evil spirits do what evil spirits do because that is what they are. You can deal with a wound better if you know it was the devil that made a person hurt you because the devil is the devil, a wolf is a wolf, and a dog is a dog. They have no other agenda than to survive and just be an animal. Humans, on the other hand, can have all types of motives for biting you. To bring this into perspective, if someone was under the influence of alcohol, you may not take offense at their words as you would if they were not intoxicated.

The higher percentage of germs that humans carry represent their increased number of ulterior motives, malicious intent, revenge, spite, or just plain old jealousy. Any of these hidden-germs-in-the-mouth motives, deep-seated hatred, or unforgiveness flowing from the saliva could pass something very detrimental or cause just a bad local infection. Paul says we need to be careful not to bite and devour one another (Gal. 5:15).

Another thought about human bites is that a child's bite is less likely to get infected than an adult bite because children can't cause damage to underlying tissue—their bites are not as deep or forceful. This is why Jesus said that we need to be converted and become as humble as little children to enter the kingdom (Matt. 18:3). Little children don't harbor ill will, malice, unforgiveness, or racism. The deep forceful bite of an adult, however, along with all the germs, can potentially shut you down with "lockjaw." So beware of dogs, but also beware of humans.

Some wounds take longer to heal than others, depending on the type, cause, location, severity, and the overall health of an individual. Thus, do your best to maintain a healthy spiritual life so that healing will more likely take place in the case of a wound occurrence. Proper nutrition is also necessary for wound healing. The Word of God must be a part of your daily diet.

Some wounds may leave bad scars after healing has completed. In this case, we have to accept the fact that we've been wounded in life, but we should use our testimonies to be a blessing to others. It should serve as an ever-present reminder that God brought us through something traumatic by His grace. We were injured and still have scars, but He didn't let it destroy us.

Sometimes we have eschar, or dead tissue, that sheds from a wound. The body, through natural process of debridement, expels or rids itself of the unclean, dead, or damaged tissue. Sometimes the body needs help, and a wound-care specialist or surgeon has to debride the wound. There are different methods, but it's all about removing dead tissue that's hindering the healing process. The point, spiritually, is that there may be something *we* consider dead in our lives, but it's actually hindering our recovery. A "dead issue" sounds like "dead tissue," with which we need help. The specialist has to assess the extent and size of the wound before choosing the method of care.

I have coworkers who handle various types of wounds. One of them told me he sometimes has to make crisscross cuts into the dead tissue and make the wound bleed, scraping the edges of it to reactivate the body's healing process. Then he applies an enzymatic cream that melts down the dead tissue gradually and removes it. Sometimes you need to go to the wise counselor or a spiritual leader who can evaluate your wound and cut into something that you thought was long dead but was covering a deeper hurt that wasn't fully healed. As with physical wounds, it may be painful, but you may have to go back and cut into those areas so that you can heal properly. This is similar to the pruning Jesus was talking about in John 15. The thing about dead tissue, debris, and slough is that it attracts bacteria or hides infection. Sometimes we have to deal with things we don't want to deal with if we want to go forward in our spiritual lives. Sin is the spiritual bacteria that infects the soul and, if left untreated, can result in further damage and even death.

One physician friend of mine told me he couldn't heal people; he just puts things in proper alignment, and God does the rest, healing from the inside out. I've had many wounds over the years, both physically and spiritually, but none as severe as those I incurred in 2015. Up to that point, I had never had surgery. I was praying and had others praying for me that I wouldn't need surgery, but I now understand. The physician was a friend who cut me open and removed something that should not have been there. In the process, he left me a wound that took longer to heal than I expected. I now understand Proverbs 27:6—"Faithful are the wounds of a friend..." The wound was in the area of my facial nerve and is still sensitive, nearly a year later. It had to happen for me to effectively communicate this message and allow me to become more empathetic toward other people's wounds. Even though for years I've treated wounds and have given pain medications, I was not really as sensitive to others' wounds until my cut. At the time, I also had a spiritual wound that hurt deeply, and I couldn't understand why. But the physical made me understand the spiritual wound. I used to tell people to just forgive, let it go, and move on, but my own wound stayed sensitive for much longer than I expected. While writing this chapter on wound care, I've been recovering from physical surgery. While discussing my wound with another physician friend, he said, "You know, it can take up to eighteen months for wounds to completely heal, longer in some cases."

Remember—wounds heal in stages and heal faster where there's greater blood flow. Spiritually, apply the blood of Christ to your wounds. He was wounded for your transgressions, and by His stripes we are healed. Unforgiveness blocks or impedes the blood flow. The sooner you forgive, the sooner you're healed. Also, you must have proper nutrition for healing to take place. The Word of God as your daily bread and sitting under good teaching can promote wound healing. Sometimes you just have to take time off from doing a whole lot, and let the Word heal you.

The Purpose of Pain

Webster's refers to pain as a localized physical suffering associated with bodily disorder, whether a disease or an injury. It also describes pain as a basic sensation induced by a noxious stimulus. Medical Dictionary Online says it's an unpleasant feeling that's conveyed to the brain by sensory neurons. Pain can be physical, emotional, acute, chronic, or cancer. No one likes pain, but it definitely is a signal to the brain that something is wrong with the body. I once shut my finger in the door of an ambulance and almost passed out. Out of curiosity, I asked my anatomy and physiology teacher at the time why this happened. He shared a similar story in which he accidentally hit his thumb with a hammer and literally did pass out. He explained that the pain was so intense that it caused a chain reaction, firing all the pain receptors in his body. The body was so shocked and overwhelmed by the pain that it shut down, causing him to collapse.

We are spiritual beings housed in a body, and we have a soul. The soul is composed of the will, intellect, and the emotions. Since pain can be emotional, affecting the soul, we'll call it spiritual pain. Listening to the "pain message" will have a great effect on one's spiritual well-being, while ignoring spiritual pain can be fatal.

Acute pain is of sudden onset and can be caused by infections, fractures, heart attacks, burns, surgeries, and childbirth. Chronic pain can be the result of various ongoing disorders, lasting longer than three to six months (e.g., sickle cell, arthritis, lower back problems, nerve damage). Finally, cancer pain also can be a category, stemming from a tumor, radiation, chemotherapy, or surgery.

Application

As mentioned, pain lets you know something is wrong. Physically, pain could indicate infection, kidney stones, or a heart attack, but whatever the reason, we know something is wrong. Thus, spiritually, when we're hurting, it means something is wrong. To find the root, we must examine the severity, onset, location, type, and duration of the pain. Is there anything that makes the pain worse or lessen in intensity? These are signs that speak to you. Pain in the chest that increases on exertion could be letting you know that you're having a heart attack or that you have a blockage that needs immediate attention. Ignoring a hurting heart that's working through the pain could be detrimental. Pain in the abdomen that's tender when pressed could indicate something acute going on inside, such as appendicitis, perforation, or gallbladder or liver problems. In a conversation, if someone brings up a certain issue in your life or a subject that makes you angry, upset, or tearful or causes you to act out, it could be a sore spot or area of infection that needs treatment.

Pain tells you to see about yourself. Not only does it tell you something is wrong, but it also tells you to go to the doctor or hospital. Spiritually, pain is telling you to go to the "Great Physician," to church, or to your minister. Sometimes it's simply telling you to move. When you're standing too close to a heater or fire, the pain is saying, "Move!" It's the same with sitting or lying in a position that causes pain; eventually you move or reposition yourself. This is one meaning of the passages of scripture where Jesus said if your hand offends you or causes you to sin, cut it off. Sometimes you have to remove yourself from a painful relationship, especially if you're at the point of sinning.

Another point is that of timing, as in childbirth. Labor pains in the spirit indicate it's time for spiritual birth, whether in your ministry or someone you're laboring with. As contractions or labor pains increase in frequency and intensity, just know that God is about to do something great or new in your life, ministry, career, church, or business.

The final purpose of pain is hope. One of the main things we check for in critical patients is the pain response. If a patient does not respond to pain at all, it usually means he or she is very critical. If the person responds to pain, it lets you know he or she is alive, and that means there's hope. If you're numb to everything around you—relationships, disasters, starvation, crime, or other atrocities—there's not much hope for you. So, thank God that you can feel pain. If you can get angry in a marriage and can still talk, then there's hope, because at least you're responding to pain. It means that you still care.

When you see people in pain or you are in pain, something is wrong. Pain is only a symptom, pointing to something underlying. The crying, anger, and fits of rage could be expressions of pain. Looking at the big picture and understanding that pain is indicating something that may not be obvious could help us be more empathetic with people. First Corinthians 12:26 says that if one member suffers, all members suffer. We should feel each other's pain to the point that we reach out to locate the source and help to alleviate it. In doing so, we inevitably help ourselves.

Spiritual STDs

Sexually transmitted diseases are referred to as STDs; STIs are sexually transmitted infections. These are infections people get from having sex with someone who is infected. Knowing how rampant sexual immorality is and always has been, these diseases are speaking volumes for God. It's amazing to me that people never develop immunity to these infections, no matter how many times they're exposed and treated.

Let's look at how and why STDs are transmitted. As a whole, promiscuity, unfaithfulness, and unprotected sex are the main reasons they're contracted, although rape or molestation can be the culprit as well. The most predominant mode, however, is some type of sexual immorality (e.g., adultery, fornication, multiple partners). I think it is safe to assume that there's some type of unfaithfulness or noncommittal attitude involved the majority of the time.

As we apply this spiritually, we see that God calls the relationship with Him a marriage or a love relationship in several places throughout scripture (Hosea, Ezekiel, and Songs of Solomon in the Old Testament). A passage in Isaiah 54:5 says, "Thy Maker is thine husband; the Lord of hosts is His name." In the New Testament, especially Ephesians 5 and Revelation 21, we find the mystery of Christ's love and the church are illustrated in the analogy of earthly love and the marriage relationship. Thus, from the Old Testament relationship of God and Israel to the New Testament of Christ and the church, all point to God's relationship of love with His people, along with the fact that He's a very jealous God who doesn't want us to go "whoring after other gods" (Judg. 2:17; Deut. 31; Ezek. 16, 23; Hos. 2; Jer. 2, 3; Jas. 4; Rev. 17, 19). Unfaithfulness to God results in spiritual STDs. We can whore after many things—false religions, idol gods, worldly wisdom, people, material things, or simply the cares of this world. The god of this world, Satan, is badly infected and is a carrier of all types of diseases and spiritual STDs. Just sneak around with him or his children if you dare, selling yourself to him, and see what you catch. Remember that God is very jealous and has eyes everywhere.

Now let's look at some of the actual diseases. There are more than twenty known STDs, but I'll touch on only a few. According to the National Institutes of Health (NIH), some of the more common types are chlamydia, gonorrhea, genital herpes, HIV/AIDS, syphilis, bacterial vaginosis, trichomoniasis, viral hepatitis, and human papilloma virus (HPV), which has more than forty types itself. Some of these infections can have a devastating effect on personal relationships or on the population as a whole. These diseases can leave you infertile, in pain, with cancer, or with some other debilitating condition, or dead. Understand that there's always a risk of paying a terrible price from being loose sexually. Therefore, whether physically, socially, financially, or psychologically, being unfaithful to God could have a detrimental effect as well.

Chlamydia

According to the Centers for Disease Control (CDC), chlamydia and gonorrhea are the first and second most commonly reported notifiable diseases in the United States. Often, people with these infections don't have symptoms. As in the natural, so it is spiritually. We have our pleasures of this world that we enjoy or things with which we're intimately involved that God forbids, and we seemingly get away with it, having no apparent consequences—but we're infected.

Left untreated, about 10–15 percent of women with chlamydia will develop pelvic inflammatory disease (PID). PID and "silent" infections can cause permanent damage to the reproductive system, leading to infertility. What does this mean spiritually? If we're too intimately involved with the world, loose with our morals, and commit spiritual adultery or idolatry, we may acquire spiritual chlamydia, leading to silent damage to our spiritual lives, preventing us from reproducing or living a fruitful Christian life.

Sometimes you may have symptoms, such as fever, abdominal pain, or discharge, but if you ignore them or don't take them seriously, you may suffer later. Also, if a woman becomes pregnant while infected, her developing fetus is at risk of infection, or she could develop an ectopic pregnancy, which could be life-threatening. Think about it: the ministry that you carry could become infected, diseased, or even cause you to die spiritually if you don't get the proper treatment. This is why it's so vital to get into the Word of God and be prayerful, always checking yourself. You also need a leader that can check you out at times.

If chlamydia is caught early, it easily can be treated with antibiotics. The same goes spiritually; treatment with the Word and prayerful repentance early on could easily treat certain sinful conditions, but if you ignore the signs or keep playing around with sin, it may be killing you silently or damaging your future. You may get so deep that you have trouble coming out.

Gonorrhea

Gonorrhea can grow rapidly and multiply easily in the reproductive tract. The most common symptoms are genital discharge and painful or difficult urination. I look at urination as repentance because of the toxins and waste being removed from the blood by the kidneys. In 2 Corinthians 7:1, Paul tells us to "cleanse ourselves from all filthiness of the flesh and spirit." Bowel movements could be said to cleanse the flesh, while urination cleanses the spirit.

Thus, if you have difficult or painful urination physically due to gonorrhea, it may be symbolic of spiritually having trouble repenting and getting rid of sin in which you have become intimately involved, hindering your intimacy with God. We must be willing to repent, as David was in Psalm 51 when he asked God to renew a right or loyal spirit within him after being unfaithful with Bathsheba.

Like chlamydia, gonorrhea can lead to PID, infertility, or ectopic pregnancy and potentially can spread to the fetus if acquired during pregnancy. It can infect the mouth, throat, or rectum and can spread to the blood and joints, potentially becoming a life-threatening illness.

Think about this: if the mouth, throat, and eyes can become infected physically, this means your ministry's vision and voice can be infected spiritually. The infection can spread to the child through the birth canal, causing blindness. Thus, the ministry you birth may not have vision or direction if you're infected. If you become pregnant spiritually, don't go back to being unfaithful to God; it may hurt or kill your ministry.

Syphilis

Syphilis can cause long-term complications and is known as one of the great imitators, because its symptoms mimic those of several different diseases. After you become infected, syphilis bacteria can be dormant within your body for years and even decades before becoming active again. If not treated, it can damage the brain, heart, and other organs and may become life-threatening. Sounds like sin, doesn't it?

Syphilis develops in stages (three or four, depending on how you look at it) with some overlapping and has symptoms that can occur in different order. One thing's for sure: the sooner you treat it, the better. If left untreated, it worsens. It's no wonder Jesus warned people He healed or forgave to "go and sin no more" (John 8:11) or "sin no more, lest a worse thing come upon you" (John 5:14), referring to the man he healed and the woman caught in adultery.

Also, James 1:15 says, "When lust or desire is conceived it gives birth to sin and when sin is finished or full-grown, brings forth death." Sin manifests in different stages, and symptoms vary from person to person, but if left untreated, it's to no good end in anyone.

Primary Syphilis

Painless sores or ulcers, called chancres, that appear at the spot where the bacteria entered the body is usually the first sign of syphilis. This painless ulcer develops around three weeks after exposure, usually in the area of the genitals, mouth, or rectum. Satan wants to infect the area where we receive or speak the Word of God (mouth), taint our testimony and areas of intimacy (genitalia), and contaminate the area of repentance (rectal or urinary areas). Painless symptoms suggest that there are very subtle breaches in our intimacy that often, as with the chancre, will go unnoticed or overlooked. This sore usually heals on its own within six weeks ... but you're still infected.

Secondary Syphilis

The secondary stage begins around six weeks to six months after exposure. You may get a rash that could eventually cover the entire body, including the palms of your hands and soles of your feet. The rash may be accompanied by wart-like sores in the groin, genital area, or in the mouth. Think about this: a rash is something that can alter your appearance and the texture and color of your skin. Often, we attempt to hide, cover up, or mask these areas, but we know something is wrong. You may cover these areas in public, but when you're in private, you peel off the layers, remove the makeup, expose your genitals, look inside your mouth, and rub your skin. You know that you're not looking or feeling your normal self. Spiritually, as you get in private and become honest with yourself, you know there's a breach in your relationship with God, and you're not pleased with what you feel or see.

Hebrews 4 tells us that we're all naked, exposed before God, and that we can come boldly before His throne of grace to receive help. In this secondary stage, God is letting you know something is not right, but you still have a chance to get it fixed. Some even experience muscle aches, fever, weight loss, or swollen lymph glands in this stage.

According to the Mayo Clinic, these signs and symptoms may disappear within a few weeks or repeatedly come and go for as long as a year. Sometimes we can get caught up in a repetitive cycle of sin and have depression, stress, or anxiety but don't really take the manifestations seriously. We are hurting ourselves more than we realize. If you sense that something's wrong, you're in a good place to get help.

Latent Syphilis

The latent or hidden stage occurs when syphilis is not treated, and it moves from secondary to this stage, where you have no symptoms. It's amazing how certain sins can lie dormant in our lives for years and later manifest, causing us problems. You just swept it under the rug, never dealt with it, never really repented of the sin, and one day, symptoms of it manifest.

During the latent phase, you may never have symptoms again. By the grace of God, you may never suffer ill effects again. Ecclesiastes 8:11 says, "Because sentence against an evil work is not executed speedily ... the heart of men is fully set in them to do evil." In other words, just because you've gotten by doesn't mean you've gotten away from the consequences of that action.

Tertiary (Late) Syphilis

By now, you may see the great correlation between the physical and spiritual disease and its progression to a very dangerous state when left untreated. Physically, this stage is characterized by severe problems with the heart, brain, nerves, eyes, blood vessels, liver, bones, and joints. Remember spiritual STDs are contracted from being unfaithful to God or having affection for something more than for Him.

Being caught up in these sinful activities or relationships and not repenting can lead to the point of no return or cause you to become totally unfruitful as a believer. If your heart is not right or your brain is damaged, causing dementia in the spirit, then you cannot please God or carry out your God-given assignment.

When the eyes are damaged, you lose your vision for ministry. Sometimes you have to go way back and repent of something you never got right.

Sometimes we can wait too long and never have the mind to get it right, developing spiritual dementia or a conscience seared with a hot iron. Nerve damage from syphilis may result in spiritual paralysis, where you get stuck in one place and never progress. Infected bones and joints that cause spiritual arthritis may signify having difficulty moving freely in your calling—too stiff and painful because of something in your past. Deafness could also occur. As Jesus would often say, people's "ears are dull of hearing" (Matt. 13:15), or if you have ears, "hear what the Spirit is saying" (Rev. 2:29). You're in a bad state if you're spiritually deaf. Syphilis in the last stage can cause impotence. If your ministry is impotent, you're not going to be fruitful or able to impregnate others spiritually.

Congenital Syphilis

If a woman has syphilis and gives birth to a child, the child can become infected. Although most may have no symptoms at birth, some may have a rash on their hands and feet. Later, they may have deafness, teeth deformities, cataracts, seizures, or die if not treated early. Applying this spiritually, the ministry or "baby" that you birth while something inside of you is not right could *appear* normal but later develop deformities, disorders, and ultimately die if not treated.

Some are born with low birth weight. If your ministry is smaller than normal, it could be because of something from your past. Pregnant women with the syphilis infection often deliver prematurely. Could your spiritual infection have caused you to deliver or give birth to your ministry prematurely, before you or *it* was ready? Sometimes women miscarry or deliver stillborn babies.

Could your intimacy with the world or multiple partners (or gods) have caused you an abortion or stillborn ministry?

Maybe you can't get your ministry off the ground because it died inside of you. Maybe your unrepentant sin from the past is the thing that hurt what you were carrying because you didn't have symptoms. While enjoying the pleasures of this sinful world but also heavily involved in church, you didn't realize you had contracted something that hurt your future. Maybe your spiritual leader wasn't thorough in checking you out. Maybe you refused to listen to a concerned leader who tried to tell you something was wrong inside of you.

Perhaps you saw the signs and symptoms but still chose to ignore them, and the infection progressed to late-stage syphilis. Syphilis can be treated easily if caught in its early stages, within less than a year. So spiritually, the sooner you repent, the better. Don't let it go to another stage. If you need to go to someone now and apologize or repent, do it. Don't let pride and stubbornness stop you and hinder your future.

Keep in mind that several different STDs can have an adverse effect on your life, some causing painful sores, burning, itching, discharge, warts, and all kinds of discomfort. Spiritually, we always should keep this at the forefront of our minds when we're tempted to be unfaithful to God. Remember also that some of these diseases may be dormant for a while, or you not know that you're infected.

This can be dangerous because you could unknowingly spread your disease to other people who become intimately involved with you. Worse than not knowing and infecting people, however, is when you know you have an STD and still spread your disease to careless or unsuspecting people. To live a double life in the pulpit, with people trusting you because you're hiding the symptoms, is something for which you have to give account to God, if you're infecting your congregation.

Part of the syphilis follow-up treatment is to avoid sexual contact until the treatment is completed and blood tests indicate you're well. In other words, sometimes we need to sit down and take our treatment before trying to minister to others again.

Spiritual HIV/AIDS

HIV is an STD with a powerful spiritual message. HIV stands for human immunodeficiency virus, which is the virus that causes AIDS, or acquired immunodeficiency syndrome. This virus attacks the immune system, causing a decrease in resistance to germs and the body's ability to fight diseases. As with all STDs, HIV/AIDS is contracted primarily through sexual intercourse with an infected person. Spiritually, Satan is the god of this sinful, secular world, and he is the embodiment of evil. If we become intimately involved with Satan or the cares of this sinful world, we can become infected, contracting spiritual AIDS.

Viruses are like evil spirits, searching for a way into your body. Although HIV can be transmitted by a contaminated blood transfusion, intravenous drug use with dirty needles, or wounds with exchange of body fluids, our primary focus is examining it as an STD. This disease is not to be taken lightly.

Spiritually, it is vital that we understand why God has always been so adamant in warning us about idolatry or spiritual adultery. As of this writing, there's no cure for AIDS; it is a most formidable foe. This sends us a powerful message about the wages of sin, which is death. We can actually trace spiritual HIV to its original source in the garden of Eden.

The original carrier as well as perpetrator is Satan. He knew he was infected, yet he talked intimately to Eve, the mother of God's earthly creation, seducing and infecting her. Eve subsequently passed the virus on to Adam. Even though they did not exhibit symptoms initially, if you had drawn their blood, they would have tested S-I-N positive. Adam lived to be 930 years old but eventually succumbed to the spiritual HIV infection.

Christ, the last Adam, came to earth to take on the virus, become infected for us, and create a vaccine against the disease of sin. The cure is in His blood. As a child, I watched a television series about a man who had a special type of blood that made him immune to all diseases and old age. It made him the target of many people, especially the rich, because a transfusion of his blood would cure the sick.

What if everyone knew the value of the blood of Christ—that it gives us immunity to sin and old age, giving us eternal life? The scriptures tell us that we're all born in sin, spiritually infected because of Adam. This is why in Christ we all must be born again. Physically, we're all still infected and are dying, but spiritually, we're renewed daily (2 Cor. 4:16). It would be quite sad to have a cure available for AIDS and refuse to accept it, try it, or believe that it has been provided. This is the same thing going on spiritually with our souls. We're dying and must believe, accept, or simply try Christ, the cure for sin, in order to be saved.

A broader perspective on spiritual AIDS reveals that we all were born infected, but accepting Christ, we received the cure. Now, as believers, Satan desires to reinfect us. Therefore, we must always guard our spiritual lives from this sinful epidemic.

How the Virus Works

AIDS is an acquired deficiency in the immune system. It's considered a syndrome, which is a collection of symptoms caused by the virus. Once HIV invades the body, it infects the cells. The main type of cells that has the most obvious effect is the CD4+ T-cell of the immune system. These cells are like a communication center or alarm system that send out signals to activate the immune system when intruders are detected. You probably can see the danger of the alarm system's being impaired. If we don't have enough God-consciousness about us to cause us to recognize sin, we can get in danger very quickly.

HIV is considered a retrovirus that has RNA (ribonucleic acid) and goes through a process called reverse transcription to form its own DNA (deoxyribonucleic acid). The DNA is the genetic blueprint for life, determining what we will become. Normally, DNA works in a certain order to help the cells make proteins and allows things to reproduce and pass on traits. When this process is altered, birth defects and diseases can occur.

All viruses must have a living host to replicate. Just as evil spirits take over people's bodies, using them for their own purposes and ultimately causing all types of symptoms to manifest, viruses require a living host, taking the host cells hostage and using its machinery to replicate. Because HIV is a retrovirus, it does things in reverse; it uses RNA to synthesize DNA. Amazingly, it steals raw material from the cell for its own purpose. In many cases, the T-cell is destroyed, resulting in impaired immunity.

The dying cell releases new retroviruses that can spread the infection. This sounds just like what Jesus said in John 10:10—the thief (Satan) only comes to "steal," "kill," and "destroy." Satan steals from us, altering our DNA, ultimately destroying our spiritual lives.

This retrovirus works by reverse transcription. Look at the word "retro," which means action that's directed backward, or reverse. Transcription is a written or printed representation of something, but within the cell it deals with the processing of genetic information represented by a sequence of DNA components. In other words, the devil wants to steal the plan of

God for your life, changing the normal sequences of things by writing his own script for you.

Ultimately, he will turn you into something God never intended for you to be, just as HIV does to the physical body. Satan, through spiritual HIV, altered Adam's and Eve's DNA. He injected his own plan through reverse transcription. But Christ, the last Adam, refused to accept his plan, telling him it's written that we live by every word from God's mouth (Matt. 4:4).

It's difficult to develop a vaccine for HIV because it changes or mutates. Satan is always developing new ways of enticing people to sin. He changes with the times. After a person is infected with HIV, it may be months or years before he or she exhibits any signs of AIDS because the immune system holds it in check. If the CD4+ T-cell count gets too low because of this disease, we can develop full-blown AIDS, resulting in all types of opportunistic infections that potentially can take us out. This is what Jesus taught us in the parable of the sower, concerning the worldly cares choking the Word of God out of our lives (Matt. 13:22).

HIV doesn't really kill you; it just destroys the immune system. Then certain types of cancers or pneumonia, like Kaposi sarcoma or pneumocystis, which are diseases the body can ordinarily fight off, can cause death. Spiritually, if your immune system has been compromised because you've been seduced by Satan and infected with the cares of this life, these earthly desires can take you out instead of Satan himself.

James 4 says we must humble ourselves, submitting to God, and then we can "resist" the devil, making him flee. Satan knows that we have immunity as long as we're submitted in our relationship with God, but if he can seduce us to turn, then he can infect us and with low resistance cause us to destroy ourselves. This is what God told Cain in Genesis 4, stating that if he didn't do "well," sin was at the door, and its desire was for him.

Spiritual HIV is out to destroy your wellness or healthy relationship with God so that other opportunistic sins can take over, leading to your spiritual demise. This is why we must use universal precautions, guarding ourselves spiritually with the whole armor of God.

Stages and Symptoms of HIV Infection

Acute Stage

The acute phase, the first stage, is when large amounts of the virus are produced in the body, with many having flu-like symptoms. Symptoms may occur within two to four weeks after infection and can include fever, rash, sore throat, and muscle and joint aches and pains. This is the body's natural response to the HIV infection.

Spiritually, if you're a believer in Christ, you should react with fever, getting angry with yourself for allowing the enemy to come in like that to infect you. You should suffer the pain of a convicting conscience. There will be a rash, altering your countenance, as with the tax collector of Luke 18:13, who wouldn't lift his eyes up toward heaven while repenting.

This is the stage to get treatment, because the sooner, the better. If you will repent during this stage, in which you're highly contagious, you may perhaps avoid infecting others from the error of your ways.

Clinical Latency Stage

After the initial acute stage, the HIV disease moves into the clinical latency stage, where the infected person has no symptoms or only mild ones. Without treatment, this stage may average around ten years. Although a person may not exhibit symptoms, he or she still is able to transmit the virus.

Spiritually, after the initial guilt and pain caused by sin, you may not appear to have any ill effects from it, but you're still infected and could unknowingly pass the disease of your sin to other people. Even the sin of indifference toward spiritual things could be caught by those who are intimately involved with you. There are times when we are wrong about something, have a blowup with someone, and then things calm down but still never really get fixed. We're still a carrier of that sin and still need treatment.

AIDS

AIDS is the final stage of the HIV infection. The immune system has been severely damaged, and you become extremely vulnerable to opportunistic infections (OIs). Your CD4+ T-cell count has fallen to a very low level. The CDC has a list of over twenty OIs that are considered AIDS-defining conditions. The CD4 cells send out signals to activate the immune system somewhat like a drum major directs the actions of a band. If the level is too low, germs may get in under the radar.

Spiritual AIDS is when your relationship with God has been compromised to the point of having a low white blood cell (WBC) count (primarily your spiritual T-cells). You can look at it as if when your spiritual WBCs are P-cells (prayer cells) and W-cells (Word cells) are low, you're at serious risk of opportunistic sins destroying you. If you find yourself yielding to temptations and doing things you previously could resist easily or you're stressing over things you used to handle easily, you may have full-blown AIDS in the spirit. There may have been a time when you could easily say no to drugs or alcohol, but now you find yourself depressed and yielding without much resistance. The list goes on, with symptoms, such as fatigue or lack of energy for the things of God, weight loss (you're not as big as you once were in God), or difficulty walking or speaking for Him. You may have caught something else that's on the verge of destroying you because of your low resistance. One could make a case that this whole nation has contracted spiritual AIDS. When we removed things like prayer and devotion from the schools, guns, violence, and drugs entered or increased. We can't leave God out of anything that we do and expect there will be no consequences.

So guard your spiritual life and get regular checkups from a spiritual leader. Make good choices. Stay connected to God, walking humbly with Him because He is your resistance. He is also the cure if you happen to fall, get infected, and develop "spiritual AIDS." His blood cleanses us from all sin.

Spiritual Heart Disease

According to the American Heart Association and the CDC, the leading cause of death in the United States is cardiovascular disease. This includes heart disease, stroke, high blood pressure, heart failure, and other conditions. When heart disease is considered separately, it's still by far the leading cause of death.

The term coronary heart disease (CHD) is often used interchangeably with coronary artery disease (CAD) and refers to a buildup of a substance called plaque within the walls of the blood vessels. The lumen, or inside of the vessel, becomes narrow, stiffens, and thickens, limiting the blood flow that brings oxygen and vital nutrients to the heart muscle. This condition of the arteries is called atherosclerotic disease. The diseased arteries actually lead to the sick heart.

Spiritual heart disease develops when something builds up in your heart's arteries that shouldn't be there and ultimately leads to a sick heart. This spiritual condition is just as dangerous to your spiritual well-being as CHD is to the physical heart.

The Heart in Scripture

As we look into the scriptures, from Genesis 6 to Revelation 18, we find numerous passages referring to the heart. We read about the "heart of God," the "heart of man," and even the "heart of Lucifer." The scriptures use terms such as a "pure heart," a "stony heart," a "strong heart," a "merry heart," and so many others to describe the condition of the heart. In order to be saved, we must "believe in our heart." With there being so much concern about the heart in scripture as well as in the health care profession, it's absolutely imperative to make the spiritual connection here.

The heart, in my opinion, is the single most vital organ in the human body. A person can be declared "brain dead" for weeks or perhaps years and be on life support, with the heart and other vital organs still functioning, but if the heart stops beating, everything dies within a matter of minutes. It's no wonder that Proverbs 4:23 warns us to "keep thy heart with all diligence, for out of it are the issues of life."

Workings of the Physical Heart

The physical heart is a muscle that pumps blood through the arteries throughout the cardiovascular system, supplying the organs and tissues with vital nutrients and oxygen. The heart has its own coronary circulation that causes it to be constantly oxygenated and nourished in order for it to function. Thus, it is vital for the vessels to stay open. If the arteries become blocked enough, ischemia occurs, which is an injury due to a lack of oxygen, and this consequently leads to a heart attack.

When a heart attack occurs, a certain part of the heart muscle dies. You've probably heard the terms "myocardial infarction" (MI) or a "coronary," which refer to a heart attack. Depending on the size, location, and extent of the damage caused by the heart attack, death could occur rapidly. This is why it's vital to take care of the heart.

It can be very frightening to have chest pains and think you're having a heart attack. Whenever there's pain in the chest area, we become alarmed because we don't want anything to happen to or go wrong with the thing that controls life. Since we're so concerned about our physical heart, why don't we have the same concern for our spiritual heart?

The Workings of the Spiritual Heart

The spiritual heart has to pump blood through our spiritual arteries to nourish and oxygenate our souls. The spiritual coronary arteries can become blocked with unforgiveness, envy, malice, anger, pride, hatred, lust, and so forth. The blood of Christ, which is the life of our spiritual body, can't flow through these unrepentant or unconfessed sins. The Bible warns us not to grieve the Holy Spirit when it tells us to be angry but not to sin by letting the sun go down while we're still angry. In other words, staying angry becomes sin, blocking the spiritual arteries, thus grieving the Holy Spirit. This is definitely not healthy for the spiritual heart.

So often I hear people say, "You don't know my heart." My response is, "You don't know your heart either." Jeremiah 17:9 tells us the heart is deceitful above all things and desperately wicked; who can know it?

People come into the emergency room with chest pain and ask me or the doctor questions about *their* hearts. Could it be, perhaps, that we know a little more about their hearts than they do? Maybe we ministers are God's spiritual nurses who know a little about people's spiritual conditions, while He is the true cardiologist and cardiac surgeon who knows the heart inside out and can repair or replace it.

Nurses are the eyes and ears for the physician when he or she is not there. The same applies spiritually to God's ministers on earth; we're God's eyes, ears, mouths, and hands to assist Him with His patients. You may make the case that God sees and hears all and is always there, so He doesn't need us, but as you read throughout scripture, God always includes us in His plans in a big way.

It's okay to go to someone who represents God concerning matters of the heart (e.g., apostles, prophets, evangelists, pastors, teachers, ministers, or brothers and sisters in the Lord). These would be physical health care workers—physicians, nurses, paramedics, EMTs, CNAs, counselors, and social workers.

There are so many people with spiritual heart problems who don't recognize the symptoms or the seriousness of their condition, just as with the physical heart. Numerous conditions can occur with the heart, such as heart failure, valve or rhythm problems, congenital heart defects, or cardiomyopathy. Any of these conditions can interfere with circulation. There's also a condition called "broken heart syndrome" that can be dangerous as well, but my primary focus is CHD.

Physical and Spiritual Cholesterol

Most of us have heard of the importance of having a good cholesterol level and that bad cholesterol levels can cause heart problems. Numerous risk factors potentially can affect the workings of the heart, such as smoking, recreational drug use, obesity, and diabetes, to name a few. While all these risk factors can be applied spiritually, it's the cholesterol analogy that really fascinated me.

It would be difficult to discuss heart disease without bringing up cholesterol, but it took me a little while to figure out the spiritual counterpart of physical cholesterol. Since cholesterol is a necessary part of our health—there is "good" and "bad" cholesterol—it was a bit more challenging to make this connection. But one day it dawned on me—pride. There's good pride, and there's bad pride. We all need a certain amount of pride in order to feel good about ourselves and to function properly.

Taking a deeper look at cholesterol, we find that it's essential in several functions in the body, such as the production of various hormones and substances that help with our digestion, as well as cell wall structuring. It's found in all cells of the human body. The American Heart Association says that cholesterol can't be dissolved in the blood and has to be transported by certain substances called lipoproteins. There are two types of lipoproteins: low-density lipoproteins (LDL) and high-density lipoprotein (HDL). LDL is often referred to as the "bad' cholesterol because it can cause plaque to build up in the arteries, resulting in a narrowing of the lumen. This can result in a decrease in blood flow to the heart muscle. HDL is considered the "good" cholesterol because it helps to take the bad cholesterol away from the heart, causing it to be expelled from the body.

Pride is most often considered bad in scripture. Most times it refers to the "lifting up" of oneself, as described of Lucifer in Isaiah 14. James 4 says God resists proud people. Proverbs 16:18 says that this kind of pride leads to destruction. But as there is more than one kind of cholesterol, there's more than one kind of pride. Just because you have pride doesn't mean you have to be a prideful person. As Paul described in 2 Corinthians 5:12, 7:4, and 8:24, a good pride would be having pride in people and desiring to make them proud. It's good to be proud of your children, but like cholesterol, too much pride can result in heart problems. He also speaks in Galatians 6 about doing your best so that you can be proud of your own work and not resort to boastful comparisons to others. Good pride causes you to do a good job in your secular work as well as your ministry. There always has to be a proper balance of the two internally. I'm sure you've run across people who have so much pride in their accomplishments that nobody can tell them anything. We can be prideful in ministries and churches to the point of boasting that we have the greatest church, musicians, or the largest membership.

It's interesting to note that cholesterol can't be dissolved in the blood. Even though we're saved by the blood of Christ, when it comes to pride, we must humble ourselves before God in order to remove it. Pride will build up in your heart's spiritual arteries and harden them, just as cholesterol makes up plaque that causes disease in the physical arteries. You will begin to resist what God or your leader is trying to tell you because you think you know it all. Just because you don't feel that your cholesterol level is elevated doesn't mean it's not. As you have to go to someone to check it and tell you that it's too high, you sometimes have to go to God or a spiritual leader to get your pride level checked. It takes a degree of humility to go to someone and get it checked. Most often, others can recognize the prideful ways in us before we can spot them in ourselves. Pride can often manifest in different ways, like boasting, stubbornness, or rebellion.

Also, the good cholesterol helps remove the bad cholesterol from the body. Good pride really makes its boast in the Lord, realizing all good gifts come from above. Godly pride removes the bad self-pride that causes us to depend on human ability instead of God-given grace. In either case, whether we have too much of the bad or not enough of the good, our hearts can become spiritually sick. A proper diet of fresh spiritual food and the exercising of what you learn can lower the bad pride and build up the good pride to healthy levels. It's always healthier to praise and boast about your God than your own knowledge or ability. Keep in mind that pride, like cholesterol, can creep up on you without manifesting symptoms and still cause damage, so don't take getting spiritual checkups lightly.

Signs and Symptoms of CHD

Symptoms of heart disease may differ between men and women. In one sense, women may be more sensitive, emotionally, than men as a whole. Take love, for instance. Women will love and love hard, putting their whole hearts into the relationship, more so than the average man. It doesn't mean that men don't love. It simply means that the signs and symptoms of their love may manifest differently. Why? Because men are wired differently. But for our purposes, I'm primarily combining the two, because in Christ, there's neither male nor female.

Symptoms of CHD may include:

1. *Chest pain or angina.* This pain is the discomfort that occurs when the heart doesn't get enough oxygen from blood flow. The pain can be sharp or burning, or it may be pressure or squeezing in the chest. Some describe it as an elephant sitting on the chest and can even extend to the arms, neck, jaw, throat, or back. The pain may increase with exercise in most people, even though some people experience this while sleeping or at rest.

    Spiritually, if you experience sudden, serious heartache in your life or ministry that is greater than usual, and it seems to get worse the more you exercise or work, you may have CHD. Perhaps you can't shake a painful experience, even while at rest or sleeping. The inability to shake what someone did to you by not forgiving that person or allowing the blood of Christ to bring the oxygen of the Spirit to your aching heart muscle could very well be an indication of some serious heart problems.

Maybe you need to apologize in order to get matters straight with a person, but instead, your arteries are filled with pride and stubbornness. Rather than humbling yourself and listening to the Spirit of God, you let the pride and stubbornness kill you spiritually with a diseased heart. Ignoring this aching heart could lead to a spiritual heart attack, where part of your heart dies. Feeling the squeeze and pressure of personal problems or ministry can be overwhelming to the heart, but the pride in the arteries can cause you to think that *you* have to be the one to get it all done. My friend, if you're exhibiting these symptoms, you may have spiritual heart disease.

2. *Shortness of breath.* The lungs and heart are responsible for carrying blood and oxygen to the tissues of the body and removing carbon dioxide, and if something interferes with this process, shortness of breath can occur. CHD interferes with the blood and oxygen flow.

By understanding how breath and oxygen deal with the Spirit of God flowing through the blood of Christ, you can see how interfering with the blood flow through unforgiveness, hatred, or pride can cause you to be "short of breath" or "short of Spirit." You'll find yourself unable to take very much before frustrations set in, causing you to start walking in the flesh.

Furthermore, God commands us to "be *filled* with the Spirit," which is allowing Him full control of our lives. The fruit of the Spirit is love, long-suffering, temperance, and others, and lacking these, you'll be irritable, short-tempered, and short on patience—in other words, short of breath or Spirit because of CHD. Remember—shortness of breath is only one symptom and could be caused by a number of different conditions.

3. *Nausea and vomiting.* Pain may extend down to the stomach and gut, causing nausea. This discomfort is often mistaken for indigestion. How often have you experienced a sick feeling in your gut because of something shocking that you heard or that happened to you that hurt your heart? Spiritually, your heart may not be healthy enough to handle, or "stomach," this experience because you've not allowed the blood of Christ to flow freely through your heart.

4. *Extreme fatigue or weakness.* If blood flow is impeded, numerous problems can occur because blood carries oxygen and vital nutrients. Therefore, you will be weak and tire easily. The same happens spiritually if your heart is not right with God. If you don't allow the blood of Christ to flow freely in your life, quickly forgiving and letting things go that shouldn't be in your heart, you will easily become fatigued and weary in your walk. You won't be as strong as you should be. You could become so weak that you actually pass out spiritually because of CHD.

5. *Sweating.* So often with heart problems, especially a heart attack, people break into a sweat, and the skin gets cold and clammy. Is there anything causing you to sweat excessively in your spiritual life? Maybe in the past, your heart was in better condition, and you allowed the peace of God to rule in your heart. But over time, trials have caused your arteries to stiffen with atherosclerosis, and now you're stressing and sweating when you should be resting in God.

It's important to note that some people have no signs or

symptoms of CHD, more so for women. This is an example of what could be going on spiritually with many of us. Just because we feel like we're fine doesn't mean we are. Sometimes no symptoms are exhibited until we actually have a heart attack, heart failure, or arrhythmia (an irregular heartbeat). This is why it's good to get regular checkups, physically and spiritually.

Spiritual Constipation

Constipation may be the most unpleasant and graphic of all subjects discussed in this book, but with an open mind, it could be the most practical, comprehensible, and humorous of all the material studied. Due to the offensive nature of much this information, I'll cut to the chase here.

Spiritual constipation, as with physical constipation, suggests that there is something inside of you that should've already come out. In this instance, the longer you wait, the harder and more painful it will be to get it out, and this is the essence of what we'll discuss. Read more if you dare, but be warned: this chapter will be more graphic.

Normal Bowel Function

To get a good understanding of constipation, we first need to look at normal bowel function. Depending on the source, your bowels should move anywhere from three times a day to once every three days. Two factors that often affect bowel function are age and dietary habits. For example, if you only eat one small meal a day, you're not likely to have three large bowel movements a day. Also, the older you get, the more your internal functioning slows down, causing the bowels not to move as often as a young person's.

The digestive system starts from the mouth and goes through the rectum, also known as the GI or gastrointestinal system. When we eat, this process is called ingestion, and the breakdown of this food is referred to as digestion. We absorb the broken-down food products and eliminate the waste products through bowel movements.

When we take in or ingest the Word of God, it's food for the soul. Jesus said that He was the "bread of life." With this understanding, we should be hungry to ingest the Word of God and digest it, breaking it down into absorbable form. When you see, smell, or even think about good food, your mouth may start to water. Your brain is stimulating your mouth to produce saliva that gets you ready to break down the food *it thinks* you're going to get. Saliva has digestive enzymes that help break down the ingested food. We should really be salivating over the Word of God with the anticipation of a delicious spiritual meal. This is also what Psalm 1 is talking about when it says we should meditate in the law day and night.

To meditate is to ponder over or think deeply. As we're open to what God is saying to us in His Word, pondering over it causes us to absorb it into our spirit man, bringing nourishment to the soul. When this process is completed, waste products are produced and eliminated through bowel movements. Therefore, when we eat regularly, our bowels should move regularly. When we have this urge, we usually go to a private place to eliminate our waste (usually a bathroom). It's probably comforting to know that every normal individual has to go through this same process.

Practical Spiritual Application

Everyone who takes in or ingests and digests the Word of God on a regular basis should have something unpleasant eliminated on a regular basis. Anything that's not needed in your life, of which the Word of God convicts you, needs to be removed and repented of, or it can cause you to become sick. As you wouldn't have a physical bowel movement in public, spiritually you would go to a private area to eliminate your waste. Of course, we don't expect any more from babies. Ingesting the Word of God should cause the urge, every so often, to push "stinking" ways, attitudes, vanities, weights, and sins out of our spiritual man. If we don't eliminate these things on a regular basis, they build up, causing us to become "spiritually constipated." In other words, we're full of something that should have already been released. When the Word of God brings something to our attention and convicts us of it, we should go to our prayer closets regularly and release it.

When people act ugly in public or show their butts, they just had a bowel movement in public. This should be done in private, where you can scream, strain, frown, and stink up the atmosphere. So often we act in ways that bring shame on us, and later we reflect on those moments with regret when we're calm. If we looked at it as if we're having a bowel movement in public, we would think twice before acting out those negative feelings. We would even be mindful of to whom we spill our guts. We should go to the spiritual bathroom where we can get rid of this unpleasantness and clean up. Don't forget to "spray" the area with thanksgiving and praise after you lay your burden down. But the spiritual bathroom is the altar or your personal prayer closet. You can also go to a wise counselor, pastor, or trustworthy Christian brother or sister.

Working in the health care field, I've learned that people get sick and lose control of their bowel functions. In those cases, they need nurses or other caregivers to be understanding and help them clean up, if needed. Loving, caring Christians, or people in general, wouldn't talk about you when they see that you need help. It's sad to be stinking up the place and refuse help—or not even know that you have a problem.

On a humorous note, I was discussing this analogy with a physician friend, and he asked facetiously, "Well then, what would passing flatus [gas] be?" I told him that it's when you want to act out but just give a mean look or unpleasant expression or body language. You just put it into the atmosphere; sometimes this stinks up the atmosphere so badly that people may think you actually had a BM. Also, when you know that you need to go but refuse to move and try to hold it, you still end up giving off an unpleasant aroma. If you find yourself in a bad mood, irritable, or touchy, you may be full of gas, meaning you may need to get away from people.

Symptoms

Let's look at some of the symptoms or ill effects related to constipation. Pain or bloating in your abdomen is one problem that can be very uncomfortable. Holding on to something that should be released can cause you unnecessary discomfort and pain. Constipation also can cause you to develop hemorrhoids (and you know how much trouble hemorrhoids can be). If you're stopped up with something in your GI tract, you can become nauseated or even vomit, resulting in a loss of appetite. Spiritually, until you release what needs to come out, your capacity to eat more is decreased, even to the point of rejecting, or vomiting, the Word. The preacher may be trying to get you to release something ungodly, according to the Word, but because you refuse, you become sick, rejecting God's Word and His moral standards.

In another instance, the pastor could be trying to feed you with a good, fresh, new Word to get you to move forward, but you can't receive it because you haven't released the old stuff, causing you to become stagnant in your walk with God. Clearly, constipation can cause some serious problems, pain, discomfort ... and even death. Please don't hold on to all the negativity of which God is trying to rid you because it could be life-altering.

Causes

Although a long list of serious disorders can cause constipation (e.g., tumors, cancer, scarring caused by inflammatory bowel diseases, nerve damage), I'll only mention those things over which we have more control.

One major cause of constipation is ignoring the urge to go. The same applies spiritually. Ignoring the promptings of the Holy Spirit to release something can cause serious pain later, which is why it's usually better to just nip things in the bud. Another cause is a lack of physical exercise. Constipation occurs when material traveling through the GI tract moves too slowly, and stool becomes dry and hard. Physical immobility slows this process. Thus, spiritually, when we're not exercising or putting into practice what we're taught, we increase chances of becoming constipated. It's always better to be a doer of the Word than a hearer in order to keep things moving; stagnation is never good.

A lack of dietary fiber can be a major cause of constipation. Fiber comes from fresh fruit, vegetables, and nuts, so fast food and processed food contribute to this problem. Spiritually, if all you're getting is "fast food" at church or wherever you can pick up a snack, this may cause your buildup. Even more so, spiritual food that is "processed" by man could cause your spiritual constipation. For example, man may process your diet with too much prosperity, love, and grace but not enough obedience, repentance, and judgment. You need fresh Word, high in fiber, which convicts you and moves you within. Even the message of God's love, served properly, should move your bowels. When we think that God's love and grace will cover us, that we don't need to repent, or that there'll be no consequences for disobedience, we may be eating too much food processed by man. Remember that constipation occurs because things are moving too slowly through the intestines. Procrastination leads to constipation. I like the sound of that.

Constipation also is caused by the lack of water or fluid intake in the diet. Water is often symbolic of the Holy Spirit in scripture. So to eat a lot of the Word of God as spiritual food but not seek to walk in the Spirit, who leads and guides us into all truths, results in spiritual constipation. The Spirit, or Comforter, is our helper. A healthy consumption of living water will help keep you regular. He convicts us and causes us to repent often (see John 16:8–13). This may be why we have so many stiff-necked, stubborn, bloated, bellyaching Christians. They need a spiritual enema of living water to flush their toilets. This could be why you're straining and crying, looking ugly at the altar—the spiritual leader is trying to de-impact you and give you a spiritual enema by the Holy Spirit's conviction. If you would take care of this regularly in private, it wouldn't smell so badly in public.

Laxatives

Laxatives are used to treat constipation, but it's always better to eat a healthy diet with fiber and drink plenty of fluids. There are various kinds of laxatives; some are considered cathartics or purgatives. The essence of their working is taking something to make you go to the bathroom, to release something. The terms *purgative* and *cathartic* are often used interchangeably, in that both deal with cleansing or purging while promoting the rapid evacuation of the bowels. Some laxatives are considered contact stimulants. The point of all this spiritually is that it's better to eat a proper spiritual diet and go regularly on your own than needing someone to give you something to "make you go." You should purge your emotions or release regularly, but sometimes someone has to stimulate you to bring about the release. You don't want to become laxative-dependent, where you always have to take something to make you go. Abuse and overuse of certain kinds of laxatives may cause a decrease in normal bowel function.

My wife and I often had to encourage our children to apologize to each other for certain offenses, but as they matured, they needed to do it on their own. It could be quite unhealthy for you if someone always has to talk you into repenting, apologizing, or releasing what's unclean within you. If they're not there to stimulate you, you could get spiritually constipated.

Get in a spiritual church that has fresh Word that moves you regularly on the inside to get stuff out of you that needs to come out. It is just that important to find a local church where the Spirit of God is moving and moving you. Also, remember that taking a lot of pain pills, like opiates, may make you feel better temporarily, but a side effect is often constipation. Spiritually, don't always look for your minister to give you pain pills to stop your pain. You can become addicted to them and become full of it, and we certainly don't want that.

Spiritual CPR

For every disorder that occurs within our bodies, God has a message He wants to convey to us or those around us. The more extensive the disorder or disease, the greater the potential impact of that revelatory knowledge. For example, Isaiah 53 speaks prophetically concerning Jesus's Crucifixion—being wounded and bruised, along with the provision of healing because of His stripes. There's great revelation in this passage concerning the completeness of our redemption from the curse of sin, sickness, and disease, but the greater impact is in the actual death and resurrection. Now, just imagine the potential of a revelation on CPR.

Let's look into physical CPR—cardiopulmonary resuscitation. You need CPR when you go into cardiac arrest. Cardiac arrest is when your heart stops, you're not breathing, and you're essentially dead. When this occurs, you need someone to breathe for you and pump your heart. You're at the mercy of someone else because you're totally helpless. This is like our spiritual condition when Christ intervened and interceded for us. Ephesians reveals how we were "dead in sins and trespasses," but He "quickened" us. Quicken means to "make alive."

The correlation between physical and spiritual CPR is clear.

We intercede on behalf of those who are dead in sin, as well as the Christians who have spiritually shut down and gone into cardiac arrest. People in either of these states need someone to rescue them because it's an emergency. As far as the lost are concerned, they are dead in sin and at any time can go into eternal cardiac arrest (the second death). However, we Christians often face tragedies and accidents along life's highways, fiery darts of the wicked, spiritual infections (sins), and numerous other problems, any of which can cause us to go into shock and cardiac arrest. This is why it's so vital to have intercessory prayer warriors. They are spiritual paramedics, EMTs, and health care workers who must always be ready to rescue those in spiritual danger. It's also a good thing for your regular layperson or Christian to know CPR, just as non-health-care-professionals often learn it to be able to assist in emergency situations.

Joel 2 speaks about the ministers weeping between the porch and the altar, saying, "Spare thy people." Abraham interceded for Sodom and Gomorrah in Genesis 18, and in Exodus 32, Moses interceded for the Hebrew children. As with CPR in the natural, most are still lost despite great effort and training. The American Heart Association gives us a great way to remember the steps of CPR. We're given the ABCs, which stands for *airway, breathing,* and *circulation*. First, make sure the airway is open, ensuring that there's nothing blocking the air from getting in, such as the tongue or something foreign. Spiritually, this is why Romans 10 says the "word is in your mouth." You have to open up and confess Jesus as Lord and Savior. The scriptures declare that no one can come unless the Father draws him or her. Somehow, we have to open the airway. Physically, we reposition the head, lifting the chin. If only we could lift people's heads and get this good news inside, to cause them to "look and live." We need to move their tongues to admit they need help.

B stands for *breathing*. In Ezekiel 37, God shows us as an extreme case where the bones were very dry and past hope, but He told the prophet to prophesy over the bones to hear the Word of the Lord. The bones, the flesh, and everything else came together, but they still had no breath in them. Therefore, God told Ezekiel to prophesy to the wind to breathe on them so they could live. Just as we can't live without natural air, we can't live without the breath or the Spirit of God.

C stands for *circulation*. The heart has to be pumped through chest compressions to get the blood circulating. We can breathe into people all day long, but if we don't get the blood to circulate, the effort will be futile. Therefore, circulation comes from touching the heart. If only we could point them to the other *C*—Christ, who shed His blood on the cross. You see, without the shedding of blood, there is no remission of sin, leaving us dead in sin. But thank God for the blood of Jesus.

I'll also add a *D*, which I learned in Advanced Cardiac Life Support. It stands for *defibrillation*. Sometimes rescue breathing or chest compressions are not the answer. Sometimes the person needs to be "shocked." There are times when a person's heart is beating irregularly, and he or she is thrown into ventricular fibrillation. The heart, in this instance, has a lot of chaotic impulses but lacks the circulation of blood and needs to be shocked out of it. Hopefully, this will start the heart all over again in the right pattern.

Spiritual Application

If you'll allow me to get personal with the spiritual application of this point, I believe it will come across very clearly. We've preached to you until we're blue in the face. As spiritual leaders, we've tried to lift your head, to get you looking in a different direction. We've fasted and prayed for you. Your life is so unstable, chaotic, and confused that you just need to be shocked. Since you won't listen or, like Jonah, refuse to obey the call on your life, God knows how to shock you with trouble: sickness, jail, divorce, financial problems, and even death.

With defibrillation, if the initial shock doesn't work, the energy level may have to be increased (depending on the type of defibrillator). This seems to be the pattern spiritually as well. God often turns up the power if the first shock or two doesn't bring us around. Jesus told the woman caught in adultery to "go and sin no more" (John 8:11). He also told the man in John 5:14 to "sin no more, lest a worse thing come upon [him]." This is exactly why people so often seem to come to God—or come *back* to God—after encountering a lot of trouble in their lives. Don't let God have to shock you with trouble in order to get you back on track.

The scriptures declare that we must all take up our crosses and follow Christ daily. In Galatians 2, Paul declares that he's crucified with Christ, yet he still lives because Christ lives on the inside. This is the perfect example of living a life to intercede for others. By applying the cross to his own life and preaching the cross to others, Paul was showing his gratitude for Jesus doing CPR on him. My friend, this is "spiritual CPR," and we must always be ready for that 911 call to assist others.

Spiritual Hypertension

One out of three Americans suffers from hypertension, also known as high blood pressure or HBP. Hypertension is called the "silent killer" because of its potential to cause strokes, heart attacks, and other serious health problems without warning. Damage can occur to vital organs silently, over a long period of time.

Blood pressure is the pressure, force, or push of blood as it flows through the blood vessels. In HBP, this pressure is much higher than it should be. If the vessels are not open or dilated adequately, resistance increases, and the heart has to pump harder to get the blood through. This is not good because something has to give, or damage will occur.

Dangers of Spiritual HBP

Relating this spiritually, if we're not open to allowing the blood of Jesus to flow to every area of our lives, we risk having spiritual HBP and damage to vessels and organs, even to the point of having a stroke or heart attack in the spirit. This can happen to us individually or collectively, as a church body or ministry. HBP is also the primary cause of kidney failure.

The kidneys are filters that clean the blood by removing waste and toxins. If vessels are damaged in the kidneys, they aren't able to remove impurities as they should. If we resist the blood of Jesus on a regular basis, we damage our capacity to remove uncleanness from our spiritual man. Paul spoke of having the "conscience seared with a hot iron" (1 Tim. 4:2), which would be the result of listening to false teachers and not yielding to God.

Lowering the Spiritual Blood Pressure

We must constantly live with a confident reliance on what Christ did for us on the cross. The book of Hebrews speaks of there being "a rest" for the people of God to enter. By grace through faith, we have been saved. This is a life of relaxation, ceasing from our reliance on human effort to please God or be right with Him. It's important to note that when you relax, your blood pressure usually goes down. Therefore, stop resisting His will and plan for your life, and let the *peace* of God rule in your heart.

Here are a few more things that contribute to HBP and ways to help reduce it:

1. *Lifestyle.* For the blood of Jesus to flow properly in your life, you must make up your mind to live a physically and spiritually healthy lifestyle. Spiritually, smoking and drinking alcohol can pollute you and get you intoxicated with the cares of this life, causing unnecessary stress.
2. *Exercise regularly.* Put into practice the things you know to do. Be a *doer* of the Word and not just a hearer. Rebelling or resisting, like Jonah, makes your blood pressure rise. The scriptures say, "Lay aside every *weight*" and the sin that besets us, and *run* the race set before us (Heb. 12:1). If we "run" for the Lord, exercising, we're certain to lose the weights and become healthier spiritually.

3. *Diet.* Develop and maintain a healthy diet, limiting sodium intake, which mostly comes from salt. The importance of a healthy, well-balanced diet can't be stressed enough. Spiritually, a healthy diet of the Word of God is essential for the soul's health. But here, the primary focus is on sodium intake; I often interchange the term with salt.

Salt: Good or Bad?

Salt so often is vilified as the demonic nutrient that's detrimental to good health. In actuality, it's essential to the body's well-being. Salt is great for seasoning food, and within the physical body, it's an electrolyte vital to muscle contraction and the conduction of electrical activity of the heart, brain, and nervous system. It's also vital in the moving of fluids in the body, as well as numerous other activities. With salt being such an essential nutrient to the physical body, and Christ telling us we're the salt of the earth, spiritually, how can it be so bad?

Of all the crucial functions of sodium within our bodies, my primary focus here is its effect on the fluid. We were drilled in nursing school with the statement "Water goes where salt is." If we take in too much salt in our diets, it can potentially cause us to retain excess fluid, consequently causing blood pressure to rise. There's been debate over this for years, but according to the National Institutes of Health, numerous studies have shown that a higher intake of salt raises blood pressure.

A Salty Application

The church, which is the body of Christ, is the salt of the earth, and water represents the Spirit of God. If we keep all the salt in the church where the majority of the fluid, or Spirit, is, this will result in an increase in blood pressure. In other words, there will be an increased pressure to perform in the church. When we go beyond the four walls of the church to minister where there is a lack of salt, the pressure to perform decreases greatly because we're inviting nonbelievers to experience what they have not yet encountered, causing them to be open or receptive to what we have to offer. However, in a church where there is too much salt, the arteries stiffen, demanding more and more of you, raising the spiritual blood pressure. Suddenly, we're consumed with debates over who is the greatest singer, preacher, or teacher. We wonder who has the greatest praise team, choir, band, or youth ministry. If they don't perform well enough, we'll go somewhere else. We're shouting, "Give me some more salt, or I'm going to another restaurant!"

Furthermore, we love to sprinkle our salty messages, songs, and testimonies into each other, those who already have enough salt. The concentration of salt is too high among believers and should be sprinkled out to the lost. Spiritual HBP may be why many of our churches or ministries are limping, causing spiritual strokes and enlarged hearts. We're retaining too much fluid among each other, and our hearts have become swollen with pride—the spiritual pride of "my" great church, ministry, choir, preacher, or even my great ability. Although we definitely need to encourage each other in our spiritual walks, we must be Spirit driven instead of performance driven. This is causing our spiritual kidneys to fail, resulting in our not keeping the blood pure.

So often we think we don't have to repent because our churches have great numbers, but this doesn't necessarily mean they're healthy. It's the same way individually. If things seem to be going well with us, we may be less inclined to have repentant hearts. This seems to have been the case of the complacent, lukewarm Laodicean church of the book of Revelation. Complacency and indifference seems to be the silent killer of spiritual hypertension.

Another example in scriptures is the early church of the book of Acts. Jesus commanded the disciples to spread the gospel, starting locally at Jerusalem but then to Judea, Samaria, and all over the earth. They seemed to be content to keep the salt in the Jerusalem area until trouble came. The Lord allowed the persecution of the church to scatter or sprinkle the salt into other regions. It's sort of like too many grown people in the house causing more arguments because it might be time for the grown kids to move out and start their own families. Evangelistic outreach lowers the spiritual blood pressure of the church by working the harvest fields and sweating out the salt to reach the lost, individually as well as collectively.

Salt is a vital nutrient in the diet, but some people are more sensitive to it than others are. Most of the salt we eat comes in processed food from stores, restaurants, and dining halls. If you eat a lot of fast food, cold cuts, canned food, and other processed-by-man spiritual foods in your church or ministry, you may be getting too much salt in your diet. Instead of fresh bread from heaven, relevant to your current needs, man will give you something he's processed, preserved, and canned for a long time. Maybe you're eating out a lot, consuming a lot of fast-food or cold cuts messages and not realizing you're not healthy spiritually.

I'm not really saying to cut back on your spiritual salt intake, although it is good to watch where it comes from. I'm just saying sprinkle it around to the places and people that need it most, and maybe you can cut back on new cases of spiritual hypertension, heart disease, and stroke. Don't let your spiritual arteries get hardened and lose their elasticity. Always be open and flexible to what God wants to do in your life, because fighting Him only hurts you. This is what He told Saul/Paul in Acts 26:14 when He said, "It's hard for you to kick against the prick or goads." It's no wonder that Paul would always start and end his letters with something about grace and peace to you. He knew we all needed grace to yield to God and peace to keep the pressure down, and he didn't want us to make the mistake that he made in unknowingly hurting himself by fighting God's will. Your blood pressure can go so high that you will have a massive stroke or heart attack and never recover. Always say yes to Christ and live.

Spiritual Diabetes

Spiritual diabetes has to do with the imbalance we have as Christians in our diet of the Word of God and the working of the Spirit. So often we fail to eat a proper well-balanced diet. As a whole, we love the sweets and fatty foods because they taste so good. In spiritual diabetes, the Word of God can be so sweet at times that we'll gorge ourselves and not exercise. The Word of God is good for us, but if we don't exercise or put into practice what we know, it will be unhealthy for us. This is what James is referring to in James 1:22, when he tells us to "be doers of the word and not hearers only, deceiving [our]selves." To deceive ourselves is to cause ourselves to be spiritually blind—and diabetes is the leading cause of blindness in America.

According to the CDC, more than eighty-six million people in the United States have prediabetes, and approximately twenty-nine million suffer from diabetes. Diabetes mellitus, or DM, was also the seventh leading cause of death listed on US death certificates. Recent health care costs for diabetes was approximately $176 billion.

Numerous complications are associated with this dreadful disease, including heart attack, stroke, high blood pressure, blindness, kidney disease, nervous system problems, amputations, and more. As we ponder these staggering facts, God has a serious message to convey to us through this disorder.

Diabetes is the first disorder that I saw as having a spiritual message when I was in nursing school back in the early 1980s. Just as I was new in my Christian walk, I was also a new nursing student. I was fascinated with both the physical and spiritual well-being of people. Relating things I studied in nursing school to the spiritual life helped make the material much easier for me to grasp.

The fact that insulin causes the body's cells to use glucose is initially what got my attention. A person has glucose (sugar) floating around in his or her blood but having no insulin will make the person sick. The food that we eat is broken down into a usable form, which is glucose, and then into ATP for energy. Insulin is the facilitator that causes the cells to be able to use the glucose.

While looking at what was happening spiritually, I knew that the Bible says, "Man does not live by bread alone but by every word coming from the mouth of God" (Matt. 4:4). Therefore, we need the Word of God as our spiritual food to live, but we also need the Spirit of God as the facilitator. The Holy Spirit is called our "Helper" in John 14–16. Just imagine, being saved by the blood of Jesus and having all this sweet word with potential energy flowing through our spiritual vessels but not having the Spirit of God to help us utilize it properly. Just as we must balance our physical diets, we must do the same with our spiritual diets.

Numerous things can be discussed concerning DM, such as the causes, complications, and the treatment of it, but my primary focus is on blood sugar being too high (hyperglycemia) or too low (hypoglycemia). I'll be relating the symptoms to our spiritual lives and watching for the danger signs. I'm more focused on type 2 diabetes because it often can be prevented, delayed, or controlled by diet and exercise.

Types of Diabetes and Pathophysiology

There are two main types of diabetes: type 1 and type 2. Type 1 diabetes is when the body produces little or no insulin, caused by a destruction of certain pancreatic cells. It could be autoimmune, meaning that the body's immune system erroneously sees the cells that produce insulin as an enemy and destroys them. (All too often, we fight the help that God has for us, resulting in our grieving the Holy Spirit.) The cause also could be idiopathic, meaning the cause is vague or unknown.

Type 2 diabetes is the most common type of diabetes. It's when the body resists the insulin or does not produce enough of it. It often results from obesity, poor dietary choices, and lack of exercise. In both types, there's an inherited predisposition, as well as something in the environment that triggers the disease. In diabetes, the blood sugar is often elevated over a long period of time, which is harmful to the kidneys, eyes, nervous system, and others body parts. The abnormally high blood glucose level is called hyperglycemia.

A bad lifestyle of resisting the Holy Spirit will definitely result in spiritual diabetes. When we're not active in God or eat the wrong things, we become spiritually obese. Obesity often contributes to insulin resistance. Insulin comes from the pancreas and is secreted out into the liver circulation, which is out of your belly, for both the pancreas and liver are located in the abdomen, or belly. This greatly correlates to when Jesus said the Holy Spirit would "flow out" of our bellies, or innermost beings. The spiritual genetics and environmental factors would be the ministry that birthed you and the things they exposed you to, which could be what contributed to your spiritual diabetes. Being birthed with certain traits that your spiritual leaders had and following their poor dietary and exercise habits could have much to do with your current spiritual health.

Other conditions result in hyperglycemia, such as trauma, tumors, infections, medications, and pregnancy. DM noticed during pregnancy is called gestational diabetes (GDM). These conditions are all considered as metabolic disorders that primarily deal with hyperglycemia and problems regulating the glucose. In these cases, the main objective is to bring the blood glucose level down and keep it as close to normal as possible.

If the blood sugar is not regulated, glucose may be at a high level in the blood, but the cells are still starved for energy. Insulin is like a key that unlocks the cell and allows the glucose to enter and generate energy. We all need energy, or power, daily. This is why Jesus said we would receive power after the Holy Spirit comes on us. The Holy Spirit would lead us and guide us into all truth. It would bring the teachings of Christ to our memory.

Glucose is stored in the liver, muscles, and fat cells. The brain has to have glucose in order to function properly and prevent cell death. It needs a constant supply of glucose from the circulation because it can't store very much. If deprived too long, there can be irreversible brain damage. With that being said, we need to constantly feed our spiritual minds a steady dose of the Word of God, allowing it to circulate through the blood, while the Holy Spirit facilitates and unlocks the Word in our minds for proper use. That's when we'll be rightly dividing His Word.

Symptoms of Diabetes

Some of the most common symptoms of diabetes include increased urination (polyuria), increased thirst (polydipsia), and increased hunger (polyphagia). These are often referred to as the three P's or the "big three" of diabetes. Other symptoms include: extreme fatigue, blurred vision, slow-to-heal wounds or bruises, and weight loss (even though you're eating more).

While looking at the symptoms of diabetes, in one sense it appears that we're all born with spiritual diabetes. Jesus said those of us who "hunger and thirst after righteousness" would be filled (Matt. 5:6). He also said come to Him if we are tired or fatigued, and He'll give us rest (Matt. 11:28). Before Christ, our vision was blurred, and we were perishing, as Proverbs 29:18 declares. The more we were eating, the more we were losing weight. We were going to church, learning about God in our heads, but our hearts were growing distant from Him because of this disorder or imbalance. We had wounds that were slow to heal until we came to Christ. He said that He came to "heal the brokenhearted" and "set at liberty" those of us who were bruised (Luke 4:18)—sounds like all of us. I guess this is why some people say that we're all still sinners but are saved by grace. Once our rebirth takes place, our sinful nature is still present, even though we now have power over it.

Hyperglycemia

As stated, hyperglycemia is when the blood sugar or glucose level is elevated beyond the normal range. Keeping it under control is the main problem when it comes to diabetes. If it stays up too long or is excessively high, it can be very harmful to the body. If our spiritual glucose, or the Word of God within us is high but we're not using it properly, it can be harmful to us as well. Whether the sugar is too high or too low, it can be dangerous. The higher the sugar is and the longer it stays up, the more serious the symptoms will become, eventually leading to severe acidosis, coma, and death. Therefore, it becomes vital to recognize the signs and symptoms as soon as possible and get it under control.

Already stated are some of the classic signs and symptoms of diabetes—the three P's, fatigue, blurred vision, and weight loss, as well as a brief spiritual application of them. Because most of these symptoms are related to the sugar being elevated, I won't mention them all again here.

Some general signs and symptoms of hyperglycemia with the spiritual application include:

1. *Nausea and vomiting.* When you're sick to your stomach and can't hold down food or liquid, it's a sign that you could be really sick. If you can't tolerate any spiritual nutrition of preaching, teaching, or fluids of a church atmosphere, it could be a sign that your blood sugar is too high. If you're sitting in church with a lot of knowledge, but the food that you're hearing is making you sick, it could be because you need to practice or use what you know properly. You may need a spiritual health care worker to help you get your sugar down at this time.
2. *Dry mouth.* The elevated sugar may cause your salivary glands to decrease the production of saliva. Have you noticed that your speech, testimony, or prayers are now dry? Maybe it's because your glucose level is too high, and you need a dose of Holy Spirit insulin.
3. *Weakness.* Not having much energy is a sign that something is wrong. When your blood glucose level is too high, you become weak because your cells are still starved for energy. To have a high level of the Word of God in you but not have the Holy Spirit working properly in your life will cause you to be spiritually weak. In other words, you may know a lot but are not allowing God to have full control in your life, or you may be grieving the Holy Spirit as we're warned about in Ephesians 4:30.
4. *Blurred vision.* This may be caused by a shifting of fluids in the body and fluid leaking in the eyes. But regardless, your vision is blurred because your sugar is too high. We

can know so much until we start to relax and rely on our own knowledge instead of the leading of God's Spirit. If you don't allow the Holy Spirit, who is your helper, to work properly or efficiently in your life, the vision for your life and ministry becomes blurred. Also, when we don't become "doers of the word," we deceive or blind ourselves.

5. *Erectile dysfunction.* This can occur because diabetes has the ability to damage the nerves and "blood vessels." If the circulation of blood is impaired, it will hinder sexual intimacy. Spiritually, this speaks for itself. If we're out of balance in our spiritual walk and lack intimacy, as is the case with spiritual diabetes, our ability to bear fruit for God is hindered.

6. *Confusion.* If the sugar is too high for too long, it can affect the brain and cause mental confusion. You can study and obtain so much spiritual or religious knowledge until you confuse yourself. This is definitely why we need the Spirit of God to have control in our lives. People who are highly intelligent but don't practice what they preach ultimately can became very confused about their lives. Spiritually, they're out of balance.

7. *Coma.* Severe hyperglycemia can cause the body to break down fat for energy, which produces toxic acids called ketones. If left untreated, eventually the body can use neither glucose nor fat for energy, causing the patient to fall into a coma. All this results in life-threatening dehydration and diabetic ketoacidosis. This is why you see people who have a lot of knowledge of the Word of God but they pass out, spiritually. You don't get a response from them when it comes to the things of God. They're in a spiritual diabetic coma, which could ultimately lead

to spiritual death. With everything you try to tell them, they can tell you what the Bible says, yet they don't do anything for God or for themselves spiritually. Many of these people never come back to church or God. The prodigal son made it back, but many don't. The Bible says Jonah was swallowed by the big fish and essentially went to the gates of hell while running from God. If you dig deep enough, you'll probably find some underlying hurt that caused them to go astray, but either way, they are unresponsive spiritually.

Hypoglycemia

Hypoglycemia is when the blood sugar level drops too low. In one sense, you would rather the sugar be too high than too low because you can go into shock, have seizures, and die quickly. Even if death doesn't occur, you could have irreversible brain damage because glucose is the brain's primary energy source. In diabetes, hypoglycemia occurs when there's too much insulin and not enough glucose in the blood. If you exercise more heavily than usual, don't eat adequately, or skip meals, your sugar can drop. If it becomes too low for too long, you can lose consciousness and have seizures.

The spiritual message here is quite clear. In order for us to keep our spiritual glucose at an adequate level, we must not overwork ourselves, and we must eat a regular diet of "daily bread" to stay replenished. Many Christians love the workings of the Holy Spirit but don't have much knowledge of the Word of God. They skip meals often, in pursuit of the Spirit. This is why you may see them going strong one moment, and in the next, they've passed out. They're out of balance. We need the Word and the Spirit just as the body needs glucose and insulin.

Signs and Symptoms of Hypoglycemia

As with hyperglycemia, symptoms may manifest differently from person to person. Some of the signs and symptoms of hypoglycemia are:

1. *Shakiness.* I've seen many people who, when their glucose drops, say that they need to eat because they feel the "shakes" or jitters. When the glucose drops too low, it causes the body to release epinephrine (adrenaline), which results in tremors or other symptoms listed here. (I also look at adrenaline as another symbol of the Holy Spirit, which empowers us to do certain things.)

    If we get too low on spiritual fuel, which is the Word of God, we become "shaky" in our spiritual walk with God. The Bible constantly tells us to be steadfast and immovable. The only way to do this is to be firmly grounded and established on the foundation of God's Word. In other words, if we miss too many meals of spiritual food, our lives become shaky, and we could start to crumble.

2. *Sweating.* I've seen many sick diabetics who were sweating profusely when they presented to the hospital. I knew that the blood sugar was probably too low. If your life gets out of balance with a lack of the Word of God, you'll begin to "sweat," or stress unnecessarily. You won't even have to wonder why if you know you've been missing a lot of meals.

3. *Hunger.* You may have already eaten but still have a strong sense of hunger. Your body is calling for more glucose when the sugar gets too low. Spiritually, you may be in a church and have already eaten but leave still hungry. It may be a sign that you're not getting adequate nutrients from

that ministry. Also, you could be hungry but ignoring the call for food, and your sugar level is constantly dropping. Therefore, it would behoove you to pick up that Bible and get a good snack or eat a hefty meal of the Word of God.

4. *Crankiness.* If you find yourself moody, touchy, or easily irritated, your glucose could be down. This speaks for itself spiritually. When you skip church or miss getting into the Word at home, you're more likely to have trouble controlling your mood or temper.

5. *Weakness.* The body has to have glucose for energy, and if it doesn't get it, blood sugar will drop too low, causing you to become weak. You must eat the Word of God regularly, or you'll become spiritually weak. The Word is our strength.

6. *Clumsiness.* Awkward or jerky movements can be embarrassing. How often do we find ourselves doing things without grace, where we can't control ourselves? We end up wondering why we did certain things that didn't make sense. Maybe your Word level was low. Keep your sugar level up.

7. *Poor concentration.* The brain has to have glucose to function properly and is very sensitive to drops in the level. You have trouble thinking clearly if it gets too low. Your spiritual mind functions by the Word of God. This is evident in Matthew 4:4, when Jesus told Satan that we live by every word from God. Even though He was hungry from fasting for forty days and had a low blood sugar, He let us know that our spiritual glucose was the most important of all for true living.

8. *Slurred speech.* If your sugar drops too low, the symptoms can mimic those of a stroke. It may sound to others as if you've had too much alcohol to drink. The brain controls

the speech and is sensitive to the drop in glucose level. When we're low on our spiritual fuel of God's Word, our speech or message becomes slurred or unclear to others.

9. *Seizures.* They are caused by chaotic electrical activity in the brain. Low sugar causes the interruption of the normal flow, resulting in the chaos. The glucose is at a dangerously low level and could result in brain damage or death. If we aren't careful, a lack of glucose or spiritual brain food could cause uncontrolled chaos in our lives. It's not that we always need to be gorging ourselves with the Word, but when we regularly leave it out of our decision making, it will lead to spiritual chaos.

    To my Pentecostal brethren, when we pursue the Spirit but leave off the Word of God, a lot of the shaking and jerking going on in the church may be "spiritual seizures." After we get up from rolling on the floor, we're still disobedient to the Word, living in chaos and confusion. It may be Holy Spirit insulin shock trying to get you to change. Sometimes He has to knock us down like He did Saul in Acts 9. You may be wrestling with Him like Jacob did in Genesis 32. His life was out of balance but when he got up, he was a changed man.

10. *Coma.* A glucose level that's too low can cause you to pass out and become unresponsive. In this case, it's considered diabetic or insulin shock. It's best that you always eat right and be obedient, yielding to God as soon as possible to avoid problems later.

Hypoglycemia, when blood sugar gets too low, is a medical emergency. You can be so critical that you can't see to yourself. Someone has to get some sugar in you very fast, or you could die. Numerous patients have come into the ER with critically low sugar levels. We've had to start an IV to stream some concentrated glucose into their veins. This is one of the miracles of medicine that never ceases to amaze me. We give the sugar, and they respond almost immediately. They don't even know how they got to the hospital, but after getting the sugar, they wake up, talking clearly and asking questions.

The same can be said spiritually. Sometimes people are so in shock with life's trials that they need a "sweet" Word from God. Sometimes they're just overworking themselves or not taking time to replenish themselves in the Word of God. They get to the point that they can't respond on their own. You have to give them a Word of hope or encouragement to let them know that everything is going to be all right. At that time, they don't need a protein meal of sound doctrinal teaching. They just need the concentrated sweets to get their emergency taken care of.

A Few More Things Affecting the Glucose Level

Hyperglycemia can be brought on by:

1. *Infection.* It can cause the blood sugar to elevate. Sin, which is a spiritual infection, can cause the spiritual glucose to rise. Keep a repentant attitude in order to keep the sugar in check.
2. *Stress.* Relationship issues, job, ministry, or financial problems can be stressful, elevating the sugar level. Let the peace of God reduce your stress level as well as keep your blood sugar at bay.
3. *Eating more than usual* (especially sugary foods). Most people love to eat, but to consume excessive meals and not exercise is definitely unhealthy. Your diet has to be balanced. Most Christians love high-carb, sugary sermons. While we all require sugar for energy and

general functioning, we don't need as much if we're not doing much for God. Seek God's balance of allowing the insulin of the Holy Spirit to help you break down and use your glucose of the Word properly.

Hypoglycemia can be brought on by:

1. *Overexercising or overworking.* If you burn off the energy, you definitely have to replenish your levels. Sometimes we're so busy "working for Jesus" that we don't give Him time to pour back into us.

    The perfect case was displayed in Luke 10, when Martha burned out and complained to Jesus that Mary wouldn't help her work. She became spiritually hypoglycemic, resulting in irritability, anxiety, and panic in the kitchen. She was preparing to feed Jesus, not realizing *she* first needed to be fed spiritually, just like Mary. It can be suggested that Martha was initially sitting at Jesus's feet, eating the Word along with Mary, but she got distracted, which then suggests that she did not eat an adequate meal of the Word. Let's not criticize Martha too harshly because we need both personalities in ministry in order to function properly. There is probably a great shortage of her type anyway. So many sit back and get the Word but don't get up and act on what they're hearing. They trust or allow the Martha personality to do all the work, while they gorge themselves "deeply" into the Word. This is an issue that will run their sugar up.

2. *Skipping meals.* Not eating adequately or skipping or delaying meals causes the glucose level to drop. You don't need to skip church or whatever means that you're being fed your spiritual meals. The Bible says we shouldn't forsake assembling ourselves together. It's good to break

bread together and share our meals regularly. In other words, we should not skip our regularly scheduled spiritual meals as we may do with our physical meals.

3. *Drinking alcohol.* This causes the body to produce excess insulin, resulting in low glucose levels. I would relate alcohol consumption to being intoxicated with the cares and pleasures of this world, causing you to expend excess energy that would lower your spiritual sugar level. The Holy Spirit is released like insulin, even more so to help keep you out of trouble while using up all the Word energy that you do have inside. It's not like the Word of God or the Holy Spirit ever gets weak or used up; it's just that God has set us up this way. He requires that we have constant fellowship with Him, and if we don't, we become drained.

Numerous complications can occur as a result of diabetes. It's even worse if you don't do your best to keep it under control. Even doing your best, there are still some complications for which you are always more at risk of developing because of it. You have to watch yourself because your wounds can be slow to heal, resulting in amputations. Infections can get you out of balance. The uncontrolled sugar can lead to blindness, kidney failure, heart disease, and numerous other problems. This is why you must take care of yourself spiritually, with proper diet and exercise and regular visits to your spiritual physician.

Spiritual Obesity

According to the National Institutes of Health, obesity means having too much body fat. Even though it is different from being overweight, which means weighing too much, we'll touch on both for the purposes of the spiritual application. Being overweight can also be unhealthy, but the weight may come from muscle, bone, fat, water, tumors, or a combination of any of these. For instance, if your heart, liver, or kidneys are not healthy, this could be the reason for your swelling or excess water weight.

Some people's frames are larger and taller than others. This does not mean they are unhealthy. Just imagine this: some people's ministries reach a higher height and cover a larger area than others. Isn't that powerful? They would be considered "heavyweights" but not overweight. Whether obese or just overweight, the person's weight is greater than what is considered healthy for his or her height.

Obesity develops when you take in or eat more calories than you burn off. Various factors may affect your weight, including genetics, high fat intake, overeating, or lack of exercise. Being obese puts you at risk for diabetes, heart disease, stroke, arthritis, and even cancer. Thus, obesity can be dangerous and a serious threat to your well-being. If this is true physically, how much more is it true spiritually?

Spiritual obesity would be the result of taking in more spiritual food energy than you burn off; in other words, being hearers of the Word more than doers (James 1:22). What could this look like? Eating the Word regularly, even gorging on it, snacking on late-night Christian television, books, CDs, and DVDs but not exercising or putting into practice what you learn. High fat intake helps contribute to obesity. Fat makes food taste really good, but the diet must be balanced. You get a lot of fat by going to big conferences. I love them, but some people have what I call "conference-itis" or "conference-osis." They're inflamed to get to the next conference and fail to get the protein of sound doctrine at a local church fellowship. If a certain preacher's large ministries come to town, they just have to be there. I'm not speaking against large or mega-ministries; it's just the condition that some people have. With some preachers and teachers having hefty-sized messages and material, some Christians are liable to go down that great spiritual buffet line and eat themselves to death. We have to remember: to him or her who know to do good but don't, to them it is sin (James 4:17). When sin is finished, it brings forth death (James 1:15). A person can go from spiritual obesity to spiritual heart disease, diabetes, cancer, stroke, or arthritis, never really fulfilling his or her God-given potential.

What's the healthy thing? We must balance our spiritual diets. Our bodies require a certain amount of fat to absorb certain nutrients, ensure proper nerve and brain functioning, protect organs, and provide energy (just to name a few). The Bible speaks of several feasts, such as large annual gatherings or holy convocations. Even to this day we continue to have large gatherings, camp meetings, and leadership conferences. We need the fat we get from these meetings in order to get our spiritual brains and local churches energized and moving in the right direction. But we can't just live off the big meetings. We need carbohydrates for energy that comes through strong preaching of the good news of the gospel. We need protein for muscle building, which is like good teaching that provides sound doctrine. We need the balance of all food groups in our diets. Any excess or unused food calories are turned into excess fat, promoting obesity, which can apply both physically and spiritually.

You must start putting into practice what you know: exercise your God-given gifts and burn some of that spiritual energy or calories that you've been consuming. You know so much, but how much are you doing in relation to what you know? Physically, if you are obese and lose 5–10 percent of your body weight, it can prevent or delay some of the diseases. How about spiritually? If you lay aside every "weight" and sin that slows you down or holds you back, and you begin to run this race with patience, you'll thank yourself in the long run (Heb. 12:1). Pace yourself and start some exercises. You've already eaten enough to save the world.

Sometimes you're required to go deeper. As I mentioned earlier, sometimes you can have excess weight due to fluid retention, but the swelling could be associated with a number of problems, such as heart, liver, or kidney failure. It's important to observe the various causes of the symptoms in order to treat the problem that's causing the swelling.

If your heart is bad, causing you to be swollen or puffed up with pride, then you may need the Lord to do a transplant on you. You could need a liver or kidney transplant, as both organs deal with detoxifying the body of poisons. Some things you just have to repent and ask God to do the surgery to remove the tumor or whatever is causing the excess weight. He's the Great Physician, specializing in all areas.

Spiritual Cancer

Cancer is a dreadful term that strikes fear into the hearts of numerous Americans each year. There are hundreds of thousands of new cases and deaths reported from it each year. It's so widespread that we cannot ignore its sermon. Cancer disrupts families and alters plans, causing much pain and suffering.

Although great strides have been made in treating cancer, to date there's still no across-the-board cure for the disease. Cancer is a subject we don't like to think about, but if you'll travel with me a while, you may learn to diagnose it when you're exposed to it in church, ministry, or even within yourself.

Cancer is a term used for diseases in which abnormal cells divide without control and are able to invade other tissues. There are more than a hundred different types of cancer. Most are named for the organ or type of cell in which they start (i.e., cancer starting in the liver is called liver cancer). Cancer is a genetic problem dealing with changes in a person's DNA. The information programmed into a person's cells becomes altered and causes something to grow in a way that it shouldn't.

Looking at this disease spiritually, abnormal and uncontrolled growth in a ministry or church body just might be a sign of something wrong, like "spiritual cancer." In other words, just because your church is growing rapidly doesn't mean that it's healthy growth. These types of abnormalities started because of the changes in the original plan that God had for us, which is mentioned in the book of Genesis. Listening to the serpent and eating from the tree of knowledge of good and evil damaged and altered our DNA that God had initially programmed into us. As born-again believers, we still have the old nature within that contains damaged DNA that we must constantly contend with. Even looking at the fact that cancers are often named for the organ or system they start in, you may see an overall healthy church until some selfish "tumor" wants to stand out in the music ministry. Next, it invades other departments or ministries of the church, and the whole work becomes sick.

■ The Pathogenesis of Cancer

All cancer is genetic, with a small portion being inherited. It all starts with the DNA (deoxyribonucleic acid), which contains the information that directs all the activity of each cell. The DNA is the same in all the body's cells. DNA exists in a double helix strand that resembles a ladder. Each strand is made up of numerous building blocks called chemical bases. There are only four bases, which are adenine (A), guanine (G), cytosine (C), and thymine (T), but they are rearranged in numerous ways. The sequence of these bases determines the message, just as the arrangement of letters determine words and sentences. The order of things encoded into your DNA is what determines everything that you are or become. DNA has the ability to make copies of itself, and each strand can be the blueprint for the order of bases for the next strand of DNA. Whenever cells divide, things must be copied exactly the same for the next cell. An error in the copying process is what causes disease.

A gene is a working subunit of a DNA molecule, carrying a particular set of instructions that allows a cell to produce a specific product. Different genes have different functions, but the heart of their function is carrying instructions for building proteins. The information from a gene is copied base by base from a DNA strand into a strand of mRNA (messenger ribonucleic acid). The mRNA goes out of the nucleus and directs the building of proteins from amino acids. All this is vital because if instructions are not carried out properly, it can result in a disorder such as cancer. God has given us certain instructions to do things in an orderly manner, and if we don't do as He instructed us, it can result in our having spiritual cancer. It originally developed in us in the garden when Adam and Eve sinned, but another example of this is Saul's not following the specific instructions that Samuel gave him from God (1 Samuel 15). He did things his own way, and Samuel told him that his rebellion was as the sin of witchcraft. The instructions had been handed down to Saul by Samuel but were from God. The prophet Samuel had the gene from God's overall DNA plan and was trying to convey it to him in order for Saul to be the messenger RNA that would direct the activity of his people. However, Saul dropped the ball in doing things his own way, for he made excuses and was ultimately stripped of the kingdom. But thanks be to God for sending us His only son, Jesus, who was the only one who ever did everything perfectly, according to the Father's plan. As a result, He repaired the error in our genetic makeup.

In the case of spiritual cancer in a church, there needs to be some rules to go by. If a person is a highly gifted musician or talented singer but has behavior unbecoming of a believer, he or she still has to be held accountable like the other members of that body. On a football team, a star player can become cancerous to the team because the person is not disciplined or is consumed with his individual stats so much so that the entire team suffers.

Free Radicals and Cancer

I'm sure you've heard about free radicals and antioxidants. Although much of this is theory, many studies have been done in the direction of evidence for the potentially harmful effect of free radicals and the benefit of antioxidants. "Free radical" is suggestive of something roaming around freely in your body with the potential to cause damage. They are the by-product of the metabolism of the food and oxygen we take in to get energy. When substances react with oxygen, the process is oxidation. Burning sugar for energy produces free radicals. They are unstable molecules that are electrically charged but missing an electron. They go around looking for their missing electron and will "steal" one from another molecule in order to be whole or complete. They end up setting off a chain reaction when this occurs, damaging cells and causing others to become unstable. In the simplest terms, antioxidants are the nutrients in foods and vitamins that help block the harmful effect of these free radicals while interrupting this chain reaction. It's expected that we'll have some free radicals in the body, but having high levels of them can contribute to health problems, such as heart disease, diabetes, cancer, and other inflammatory conditions. Certain things in our environment can contribute to high levels of free radicals, like pollutants, toxins, alcohol, and cigarette smoke. Stress, unhealthy diet, or injury also could cause a rise in the free radical levels in our bodies. When we have more free radicals than antioxidants, it causes a state known as "oxidative stress," which can result in severe damage or cell death. It is essential to have a healthy balance of both antioxidants and free radicals. In our spiritual lives, it's also essential to have a balance of these. Just by eating and breathing in oxygen for energy, we cause free radicals to be produced. The same goes on in the spirit realm. The Spirit that Christ breathed on us and the Word of God being our daily bread means free radicals will be a by-product. All types of people will pop up in church bodies with missing electrons, saying that God told them to do certain things. They are free radicals; they leave a trail of damage behind, hurting people, churches, or ministries while trying to "find" themselves.

To better understand how free radicals cause damage within our bodies, we need to look at it from the molecular level. Everything, including our bodies, is made up of atoms and molecules. Atoms are made up of particles called protons and neutrons at the core, while electrons are revolving around them like planets in the solar system, going around the sun. Two or more atoms link together and form molecules. The free radical is a highly reactive molecule that's unstable because it's missing an electron. They may be useful in the immune system to help fight infection but can be unhealthy if the level is too high. You may have encountered a few "free radicals" in the church or society who are missing an electron or two. They go around stealing from others and causing damage while trying to find their electron to make themselves complete. If they steal an electron from another molecule that isn't supposed to lose it, that molecule can become a free radical as well. This could damage DNA and is what contributes to cancer. Free radicals are selfish, free-spirited people who are incomplete and will take from anyone in order to make themselves complete. People like this are at risk of causing cancer in the church, in society, or within an organization, a business, or even on a sports team. Remember—DNA deals with information that directs all life, and if someone's DNA is damaged, his or her entire perspective and life can be thrown off course, physically or spiritually.

Antioxidants, on the other hand, are the molecules that step in and give or donate an electron to the free-radical molecule and stabilize it. When they give an electron, they don't become unstable. This may be why Jesus said, "It's more blessed to give than to receive." It's good to have a great number of people who are givers in a ministry—those who are willing to sacrifice for the good of the body, people who will give up something in order to stop a negative chain reaction caused by "free radical" believers. We need fellow believers who understand what's at stake when people who are not whole are searching to find themselves or their missing electron. Antioxidants are the stable givers among us who are secure with themselves in God and understand that if they lose an electron or two, it doesn't take away from who they are. In fact, they "live to give and give to live."

On a nutritional level, we need to eat a variety of colors of fresh fruits and vegetables in order to get a proper amount of antioxidants. Some nutritionists refer to it as "eating the rainbow." This is also suggestive of eating a well-balanced diet of the Word of God. It may also involve eating some things we don't like or that we're not used to eating. Revelation 22:2 speaks of the tree of life (trees on each side of the river of life) in heaven bearing twelve kinds of fruit, with leaves that are for healing. I think the variety of fruit we need to consume for our spiritual well-being starts here on earth. As long as we live and do the work of God, we're going to have free radicals among us. We just have to have enough antioxidants among us to counteract their destructive effect.

Other ways to control the free-radical levels include avoiding stress by allowing the peace of God to rule in your life. Allow peace to rule within you so that peace will be in your home, church, or any relationship you may engage in. Since Satan is the "prince of the power of the air" (Eph. 2) or atmosphere, avoid breathing in places where he's polluted the air with negative influences. Sometimes you have to avoid certain people if they are influencing you to sin. If you have to turn the television to a positive channel or avoid certain things on the social media circuit. Do what you must to prevent rises in free-radical levels in your personal life. You definitely need to avoid certain unhealthy indulgences, such as alcohol consumption and cigarette smoking. Any of these factors or practices can contribute to the cause of cancer. It is the case physically as it is spiritually.

Normal vs. Abnormal Cell Growth

Our bodies are made up of millions of living cells. Normal body cells grow, divide, and die in an orderly manner. Normal cells divide faster in childhood, allowing for growth, but most only divide to replace worn-out or dying cells once they become adults. Cell division also occurs to repair injury.

The church, which is the body of Christ, is made up of millions of living souls—that would be us, the believers. First Peter 2 says we're "living stones" in God's building. We're growing—increasing within the body of Christ, and dividing—replacing those who are old or worn-out in ministry, passing the torch. We replace or repair injured parts within the body.

Cancer is the out-of-control cell growth in certain parts of the body. This is abnormal, and instead of dying, cancer cells continue to grow and form new abnormal cells. These cells can invade other tissues, something normal cells cannot do. This growing out of control and invasion of other tissues is what makes a cell cancerous. When people refuse to "die" to what they want for the good of the body, this is spiritual cancer. The Bible even tells us to put to death or mortify certain desires lurking within us (Col. 3:4).

Spiritual Metastasis

Cancer cells often travel to other parts of the body where they begin to grow and form new tumors that replace normal tissue. This is called *metastasis*, a term none of us like to hear. Some people love to travel from church to church forming new spiritual tumors. They love the idea of growing rapidly with the newest church or ministry in town. That particular church is so excited about the new members, or new growth, that they fail to check to see if it's cancerous. So often, they're put into leadership too soon because they have a gift but didn't get a scan or biopsy done. In a position of authority, they are often given the right to spread their cancerous lifestyle and teachings rapidly. Remember—not all fast-growing ministries or churches are cancerous, but one has to check the foundation or doctrine of these organizations, especially that of some of the so-called seeker-friendly or prosperity ministries.

When people refuse to be subject in one ministry and invade other ministries in a church body, or they leave and go to another church, they become a cancer cell there. A tumor would be a group of abnormal cells or people who take "their group" with them, splitting that church for their own selfish reasons. They do it in the name of growth but to the detriment of the whole body. Keep in mind that tumors and cancer cells are growth also but abnormal growth.

DNA Damage

Cells become cancer cells because of damage to the DNA. DNA is the blueprint or information center found in all cells of the body except the red blood cells. (Amazingly, the red blood cells don't have DNA, suggesting that it doesn't matter about our information or obedience to the letter of the law concerning our salvation. The blood of Christ saves us, despite our understanding the details and perfect copying of instructions, so hallelujah!) The DNA directs all the cell's actions. If DNA gets damaged in a normal cell, it's either repaired or it dies. In cancer cells, the damaged DNA isn't repaired, but the cell doesn't die like normal cells do. This cell goes on to make new cells with this same damaged DNA.

If a person gets hurt, damaged, or offended, they must get repaired or die to what they want. So often, people are offended in church and never see their need to be repaired. The DNA, which directs and controls all their actions, is now faulty but continues to be copied. Other souls come in as a result of this person with the same erroneous teaching, belief system, or doctrine that directs their actions as well. Bear in mind that offense can come from actual or perceived injustice. It all started from one cell that didn't get repaired and refused to "humble" itself. Whole cancerous denominations have been born with this faulty DNA and have grown rapidly.

DNA damage can be inherited, but most is caused by mistakes that happen while normal cells are reproducing or by something in the environment. Spiritually, we're exposed to things that damage us, people we're around, natural things that our flesh loves—any of which can alter our DNA and cause us to error. Eve was seduced and damaged by the serpent in the garden, and this is still happening to us today. Her desire to get ahead physically but illegally caused her to get behind spiritually. Satan deceived her with inaccurate information.

Mistakes in normal cell reproduction that can cause cancer could be someone's misquoting or misinterpreting scripture while leading a person to Christ. Although that person may be sincere and genuinely get regenerated, some of the information can be passed down to him or her erroneously during the process. Note that I said "re-'gene'-erated"—*new* spiritual DNA—but some mistakes passed on. This is why grace is so precious to us. God often blesses us, even while we're off course.

Signs and Symptoms of Cancer

Some of the general signs and symptoms of physical and spiritual cancer are as follows (note that having any of these signs or symptoms doesn't mean you have cancer, but it's good to know them anyway):

1. *Unexplained weight loss.* Most Americans are overweight with many attempting to lose weight, but losing weight unintentionally or without understanding why could be a problem.

    Spiritually, if you're getting smaller in your ministry, personal relationship with God, or your fellowship with others but can't explain what or why it happened, it could be a sign that something is wrong. If you know that you don't carry as much weight as you once did or are not as big as you once were in the things of God, it could be a sign of spiritual cancer.

2. *Fatigue.* This is not the normal tiredness or exhaustion from extreme work or exercise; it's an unusual weariness.

    There's a normal tiredness that comes with ministry, dealing with people and their issues. Sometimes our personalities cause us to overwork ourselves like Martha in Luke 10, in which case, becoming exhausted at times is expected. But if you're fatigued for no known reason, it may be a sign of spiritual cancer. If you find yourself just tired of church, religion, people, and the things of God in general, for no obvious reason, you could have a major underlying problem. Cancer in the spirit can be just as draining as it is to the physical body.

Since cancer is genetic and deals with mutations and errors in information, maybe the way you're looking at church and people is wrong. Maybe the information in your head has become altered by an injury in your heart. In other words, you got hurt by a person or people in ministry, and it altered your DNA. As a result, you're now weary of people and no longer look at them as souls. In carrying out ministerial assignments and living a Christian life, interacting with church people, fellow believers, and people in general is inevitable, but if you find yourself unusually tired of people, you could have spiritual cancer.

3. *A sore that doesn't heal.* If kept clean, most sores in relatively healthy individuals heal fairly rapidly. If you have a sore that doesn't heal in a few days or weeks, it could be cancerous. A sore is essentially any open lesion and is usually tender, achy, or painful.

   An area in your life that's painful or sensitive when touched or pressed on could be a sore in the spirit. If you find yourself still getting angry, guarding a certain area in your life after an extended period of time, it could be cancerous.

   If a lesion is malignant, it's not going to get better but will eventually invade other tissues unless treated. The cancerous sore spreads when you constantly tell others how you were done, speaking negatively longer than usual about an incident or person. This could be a sign that you need treatment before the cancer destroys you spiritually.

4. *Persistent hoarseness.* It's an abnormal voice change, resulting in a raspy, breathy tone or straining to speak normally or clearly. Hoarseness can be caused by several things,

including sinusitis, smoking, overuse of the vocal cords, viruses, or bacteria causing infection and inflammation. If it lasts longer than two weeks, it should be checked out by a physician. It could be a sign of laryngeal or other cancers affecting the vocal cords (also called vocal folds).

There's a serious application to us, individually and collectively as a body. When the message of a church has become unclear or it becomes a strain to get our voices heard for God or by God, it may be because of cancer. It may be because we've gotten away from our first love or have become lukewarm, as the churches of Revelation.

Isaiah 58:4 and 2 Chronicles 7:14 tell us how the wicked ways that we have could be hindering our voices from being heard on high. Perhaps it's the selfish wickedness of spiritual cancer that has us hoarse before God. Maybe it's the compromise of the true gospel in order to draw more people into our ministry, leading to great error. Your stand on certain lifestyle topics has now become obscured. You could be trying to befriend everyone when you know what God has said in His Word about friendship with the world. Your prayer voice as well as your testimony is now hoarse because it's unclear what you actually stand for spiritually. But God can heal that spiritual cancer in your voice box.

5. *Changes in bowel or bladder habits.* If you don't eliminate waste daily as you should, it not only makes you feel bad but also signifies that something's not right. Bowels and bladder both deal with ridding the body of something that needs to be released.

   Therefore, if you were once regular in your prayer life, daily releasing things through repentance to God and forgiveness of people's trespasses, but all of a sudden you're irregular, this could be an early sign of disease. The sooner you notice the changes and treat it, the better off you are.

6. *Problems eating.* Difficulty swallowing, pain, or discomfort after eating, or loss of appetite could be signs of cancer. You've probably seen people lose their appetite with cancer and ultimately lose a lot of weight because of it. The same thing happens to us spiritually.

Spiritual cancer will steal the very appetite and hunger for the things of God from your soul. You'll find yourself having a difficult time swallowing the Word that your leader is feeding you. Even when you do swallow it, it will cause you a lot of discomfort. You'll begin to think the pastor or teacher is picking on you, all because your DNA got damaged somewhere, and mutations (changes) occurred within you. It could be the same Word that you had been eating, but it's now making you sick. Even though there can be numerous other causes, you have to consider the likelihood of spiritual cancer.

7. *Unexplained fevers or night sweats.* The body normally reacts to germs by the immune system, causing an inflammatory response. Several things can cause night sweats, ranging from anxiety to HIV. However, cancer is also a possibility with the symptom of unexplained sweats or fever.

The spiritual application of fever is that your temper is rising, and you're getting "hot" or angry. Night sweats are suggestive of your being upset and stressed out during the time that you should be resting, sleeping, and relaxing. You're "sweating" something that you previously had under control. This could be because your DNA is damaged from some hurtful, harmful experience, and you're now stressing with spiritual cancer.

A bad relationship or engaging in activities that you were warned about being hazardous to your spiritual health could be what altered your DNA. You could know that a person is not right for you but still be determined to stay with that person to prove others wrong or because you feel you have to have that person. You may not be sweating in front of people but are just having night sweats because of spiritual cancer. They've got you hot, always running a fever, and you don't know why. You know in your heart of hearts that something is wrong; therefore, you should get checked out if this happens to you before it destroys you.

Conclusion

There's so much more that can be discussed because of the magnitude of this disease. Even with constant and current research on cancer, new information constantly is learned, but there's so much out there that we don't know. We already have the cure for spiritual cancer, and God willing, we'll one day have a cure for the many types of physical cancer as well. In the meantime, watch for the above signs and symptoms and get frequent checkups. Have your leader scan you with the Word of God at times. As said in Hebrews 4:12, the Word of God is alive and cuts down to the bone marrow of the soul and spirit. It will biopsy you and tests the very motives of your every cell if you'll sign the permit. It will also do the surgery to cut out of you whatever needs to be removed. The Holy Spirit will do the radiation or chemotherapy on you to destroy the things that are inoperable without damaging the good cells.

Spiritual Lupus

There's such a powerful message in the condition of lupus. It is deep and complex, and it brings out many major truths. I've taken care of many patients with lupus over the years and know many people who suffer from it. I just know God is speaking to the body through this disease.

There are different forms of this disease, but for our purpose, we'll discuss systemic lupus erythematosus (also called SLE or lupus). Discoid lupus is limited to the skin, but SLE involves internal organs. Lupus is a chronic, inflammatory autoimmune disorder. It's a disease of the body's vascular and connective tissue that can affect multiple organs and body systems. With lupus being an autoimmune disease, the cause is not fully known. It is understood that there is a problem with the body's normal immune response. The immune system normally protects the body against harmful substances. In a person with an autoimmune disease, the immune system can't tell the difference between harmful and healthy substances. The immune system becomes overactive, attacking healthy cells and tissue. This makes for a very powerful spiritual truth.

Application

As Christians, in church and ministry, we often attack, fight, or hurt ourselves spiritually because we can't tell the difference between good and evil. How does this sound: the body fighting against itself or seeing its own members as the enemy. This sounds a lot like Galatians 5:15, which says, "But if you bite and devour one another, beware lest you be consumed by another!"

By backbiting, gossiping, slandering, and condemning each other, we hurt ourselves because we are the body of Christ together. Church members who engage in this type of activity are sick and have a disorder in the spirit—spiritual lupus. Eventually, by not recognizing this condition, we destroy ourselves, individually and collectively. Although the true body of Christ can never be destroyed, we can see people hurting each other and falling away from church and, ultimately, from God. We also see the strife that causes church splits and the total collapse of church bodies, all because we have a disorder that causes us to not know the difference between good and evil.

So often the kidneys shut down, and the patient has to go on dialysis or get a transplant. Kidneys are filters that remove toxins and waste from the body through urination. Spiritually, if the enemy can cause us to fight or wrestle against flesh and blood instead of recognizing our real enemies—the unseen satanic forces of darkness—then he can cause our spiritual kidneys of prayer and intercession to shut down. If we stop praying for each other and stop repenting regularly, the spiritual toxins of sin ultimately will destroy us. This is just one system, but lupus can affect or cause inflammation of the connective tissue in practically every component of the body, including the brain, lungs, skin, and the blood. I look at the inflammation of the connective tissue as strife, hot tempers, or any anger disrupting the unity in the body of Christ, such as arguments breaking out for seemingly unknown reasons. If we're believers in Christ, we can't get away from the fact that we're all connected. Remembering how dangerous and deadly physical lupus can be can help keep us unified spiritually.

Lupus is a chronic disease and affects each person differently. This makes it difficult to diagnose because many of the symptoms could have other causes. Just as it is in the physical, so it is in the case of spiritual lupus. Many of the symptoms of pain, fever, and strife—which represent anger and strife—could be caused by several different conditions spiritually.

Let's examine some of these symptoms to see how they may apply as spiritual lupus:

1. *Fatigue.* If you find yourself tiring easily in your walk with God, being inconsistent or easily frustrated, you may have spiritual lupus.
2. *Fever.* If you find yourself angry with your brother or sister in the Lord for seemly no reasonable explanation, you may have the disease.
3. *Hair loss.* The Bible says a woman's long hair is given to her for a covering and it's a glory to her (1 Cor. 11:15). If we, as individuals or the church, start to lose the glory the church once had, it may be a sign of spiritual lupus.
4. *Rash.* This could occur when our appearance changes, and the face of our ministry, or central message, is unclear because our lives are contradictory.
5. *Loss of appetite.* Do you find yourself not as hungry for God or the things of God as you once were?
6. *Weight loss.* You're not as big or heavy in God as you once were.
7. *Swollen or painful joints.* Have you become a stiff, slow-moving Christian who is difficult to work with? If you're always negative and fighting against progress or what someone else is trying to get accomplished in

ministry, you may actually be the source of pain in the body—spiritual lupus. Sometimes we cause damage even when we're trying to help. We may be overly critical or judgmental of our brother or sister. This is what is meant in Ephesians 6 when Paul says that fathers should not provoke their children to anger because as a result, the connective tissue is affected, and there's not a good working relationship. There's inflammation or animosity between joints that are supposed to be connected and working smoothly together. This is equally true in many areas of ministry. Don't think you always have to be the one to "fix" everybody or everything.

A few things to help manage spiritual lupus are as follows:

1. *Rest.* Rest in the Lord. Wait on Him, and He will renew your strength.
2. *Eat a healthy diet.* Take in your spiritual daily bread.
3. *Regular exercise.* Do not be just a hearer but also a *doer* of the Word.
4. *Manage your stress.* Allow the peace of God to rule in your heart.

While there may be no cure for the physical disease of lupus to date, God is the healer of all diseases, whether physical or spiritual. As far as spiritual lupus is concerned, if we would always keep in mind that we're all a part of Christ's body and ultimately connected to each other, this should heal us or prevent us from developing it in the first place.

Spiritual Dehydration

Spiritual dehydration is another very interesting condition. Physical dehydration paints a very vivid picture of what's happening to us in the spirit. Physical dehydration is not having enough water in the body. It can be mild, moderate, or severe. Ephesians 5 tells us to "be filled with the Spirit." So if we can be filled with the Spirit, then we can be low in spiritual fluid, or dehydrated. Water is often symbolic of the Spirit of God in scripture. John 7:37–39 says,

> In that last day, that great day of the feast, Jesus stood and cried saying, If any man thirst, let him come unto me and drink. He that believeth on me as the scripture hath said, out of his belly shall flow rivers of living water. (But this spake He of the Spirit that they that believe on Him should receive: for the Holy Ghost was not yet given, because that Jesus was not yet glorified.)

The Importance of Water

Although a person can live several weeks without food, water is such a vital nutrient that one can only live a few days without it.

Water is vital for metabolism to take place in the body. Metabolism is essentially all the chemical reactions that take place within the body's cells. It's the process of converting food and water into energy to keep us alive. Without enough water, there will be no metabolism, resulting in death.

Other functions of water include protecting organs and tissues, moistening tissues, regulating body temperature, carrying nutrients and oxygen to cells, and removing waste from the body. Therefore, without water, the physical body dies, and without the Spirit of God, the soul dies.

You can see how vital water is in regulating activities and sustaining life within the body, but it is also essential for everything on the planet to function. Water is required for cooking, bathing, washing, and everything else in life. It is just as serious to have this same perspective concerning the necessity of the Spirit of God in everything we do spiritually.

Causes of Dehydration

If you lose too much water or don't drink enough fluids, you will become dehydrated. All healthy individuals lose fluid daily through urination. There is also the loss of fluid through insensible water loss. This is fluid that is not noticed by the person because it's evaporating through the skin and the respiratory tract, as well as loss through feces. This tells me that when we live a godly life, we pour out God's Spirit to bless others as well as lose fluids while maintaining what we have. If we don't replenish our fluid loss regularly, we may become dehydrated spiritually.

Some of the causes of dehydration include the following:

1. *Excessive sweating.* Whether sweating from vigorous activity or hot weather, you can lose too much fluid. If

you work hard for God and don't replenish the fluids, you may become spiritually dehydrated. Becoming heated from the fiery trials of life or being stressed can cause you to sweat excessively, losing fluids that need to be replenished.

Sometimes we're so busy working for God that we forget to take time to drink enough spiritual fluids. When a person gets severely burned, replacing fluids is a vital thing in the hospital. We can get so burned from trials or bad relationships that we can lose fluids, rapidly becoming volume-depleted in the spirit.

2. *Fever.* It can be caused by infections, whether bacterial or viral. Fever is an inflammatory response of the immune system. It's good to get heated and have this response to something that shouldn't be in your life. It could be in the church or in society, but you must keep in mind that high fevers cause you to lose more fluids, and you could become spiritually dehydrated. If you find yourself upset by something or with a prolonged spiritual fever, make sure you drink plenty of spiritual fluids.

3. *Vomiting or diarrhea.* When something doesn't agree with your system, the body may react violently to expel it by vomiting, diarrhea, or both. Bacteria, virus, food reaction, or certain bowel problems could cause the reaction. Either way, you lose excess fluids with vomiting or diarrhea.

If you encounter sin or evil, it's a normal spiritual reaction to throw it back up, expelling it from your life. Some of these sins can cause you to lose a lot of fluids, so you must be alert to prevent dehydration. It could be contaminated spiritual food from a ministry or preacher that causes you to become sick. Also, you can have a bad reaction to the Word of God because you don't agree with the truth your leader is feeding you. He may be sincerely trying to help you, but you react violently, rejecting what he's teaching you or just letting it run right through you.

We sometimes refer to diarrhea as having the runs or the back-door trot. Be careful of the Word causing you to have the runs and making you run out the back door while the minister is teaching you. Sometimes it just takes time to get over a virus while replenishing your spiritual man with plenty of fluids.

4. *Increased urination.* Although diabetes and medications can make you lose excess fluids, urination removes waste or impurities from the body. In a spiritual sense, you may think of repentance and purifying your emotions. But if you find yourself constantly going to the altar in repentance or crying excessively, it can be emotionally draining, resulting in excess fluid loss, or spiritual dehydration.

Signs and Symptoms of Dehydration

Some signs of mild to moderate dehydration may include the following:

1. *Thirst.* You become thirsty when your body needs fluids. A place in the brain is signaled to cause thirst. If you are low in spiritual fluid, your soul has a craving for the Spirit of God. There are times we don't recognize that we're low spiritually but may find ourselves thirsting for something. In an attempt to fill this void, we try to satisfy the craving with various things when, in fact, the only thing that quenches this thirst is the Spirit of God. This is an early sign.

2. *Dry or sticky mouth.* Physically, a dry mouth speaks for itself, but spiritually, our thanksgiving and praise may become dry if we lose too much fluid. When we should be opening our mouths with praise to our awesome God, our lips are stuck together, lacking the moisture of the Spirit. Please don't ignore this sign. Even a whole church can become dehydrated, resulting in dry sermons, dry prayers, dry praise and worship service, and so forth. Don't wait on the rest of the congregation; start by doing what you need to do yourself to get refilled.
3. *Headache and muscles cramps.* Lack of water can cause pain and discomfort. I don't have to tell you how much pain and discomfort it causes you when you're spiritually deficient.

A Few Signs of Severe Dehydration

1. *Not urinating.* The inability to urinate or very little, concentrated urine is a sign of severe dehydration. As mentioned earlier, urination removes waste and toxins from the body. In the spirit, little or no repentance suggests that we could be severely dehydrated. When we're no longer convicted to repent and feel no need to intercede for others, we could be sicker than we realize. This is what Jesus warned the churches of Revelation about.
2. *Irritability.* If you find yourself touchy, moody, or easily angered, it could be that you're in dire need of a refilling of the Spirit.
3. *Mental confusion or delirium.* Any time it affects your brain to this degree, it's a serious warning sign. If you get to the point that you don't know what you're doing, where you're going, or your identity in God, these are signs that

you're at a dangerous point and are in desperate need of fluids.
4. *Sunken eyeballs.* When the eyes appear to be sunken, this is a serious sign of fluid deficit. Spiritually, if you were once easy to teach and quick to learn but now sit back, looking "deep," steeped in mysticism, you're probably in need of fluids very badly. What do I mean by this? Well, there are many instances where people allow themselves to become overly philosophical, relying on intellectual knowledge rather than the wisdom of God, thus making it difficult to receive spiritual knowledge from a leader and preventing them from responding very well to the souls around them.
5. *Fainting.* Low fluid volume can cause blood pressure to drop, weakness, shock, and unconsciousness. Spiritually, if you find yourself passing out and are just too weak to stand for God, you may be severely dehydrated and on the verge of spiritual death. Go back to the fountain of living water, and drink until you're filled.

There are other signs, but I think you can see how serious this can be. Just don't wait until it gets too bad before you seek treatment. Regularly drink plenty of Holy Spirit water to stay hydrated by being thankful and speaking to yourself in psalms, hymns, and spiritual songs. Always keep in mind that being Spirit-filled actually allows the Spirit to have full control of your life, flowing through and to every aspect of your life or ministries. When we try to accomplish things on our own, operating after the flesh, we will pass out and fail.

If you're thirsty, go to God or church and get a refill. Call 911 in the spirit if you're getting too weak, dry, or confused or have trouble walking straight. God always has someone who can help you.

Spiritual Pregnancy

I've heard quite a bit on the subject of "spiritual pregnancy" but, this subject is so vast that several books could be written on it alone. And while we're limited to one chapter regarding the subject, we'll discuss everything from birth control, infertility, and rape to abortion, miscarriage, and the trimesters of pregnancy, all the way to delivery.

Before going into spiritual pregnancy, let's look into the scriptures to get a good foundation on which to build this message. We must go all the way back to Genesis 1:26–28 where God created humans in His image and likeness, both male and female. God put His own DNA into them and told them to be fruitful, multiply, and replenish the whole earth. With nearly seven billion people in the world today, I think we've done a decent job in fulfilling this great command naturally so.

From Noah's day, after the flood wiped out everyone except eight people, we were given the same command to be fruitful and multiply, replenishing the earth (Gen. 9:1, 7). God is always giving us the natural to show us the spiritual (1 Cor. 15:44–50). In 1 Corinthians 15:20–23, Christ has become the "firstfruits" of them that slept. The New Testament allows us to see that we've all been baptized into Christ, being made partakers of His death, as well as His resurrection.

John 3:3–7 describes this process as being "born again." Second Corinthians 5:17 says that we are new creations in Christ. Therefore, we are spiritually fruitful, multiplying, and replenishing the earth with born-again souls, populating God's kingdom here on earth.

It all starts with the seeds. Galatians 3:16 tells us that Christ is the "seed" of Abraham. This is also stated in Genesis 3:15, when God declared that the seed of the woman would bruise the head of the serpent. In Matthew 13:3–23 and Mark 4:3–20, Jesus teaches the parable of the sower, and in Mark 4:14, the seed is identified as the Word of God. The Greek word for seed is *sperma*. Understanding that the male's sperm fertilizes the egg of the female during the physical process of conception, it shouldn't be hard to see that God's Word is sent out to impregnate believers spiritually.

The male provides the Y chromosome, determining the sex of the child. Spiritually, God causes the pregnancy as well as determines what it will be. Just a quick thought: if whatever is birthed does not look like, act like, or talk like God, He may not be the father. Jesus said, "By their fruits you will know them" (Matt. 7:20).

There are so many passages in scripture describing us as children of God, as in 1 John 3:1–10 and Romans 8:14–21. In Ezekiel 16:4, God describes Israel's birth, saying that its navel cord had not been cut. In Galatians 4:19, Paul says, "My little children, for whom I labor in birth again until Christ is formed in you." He is describing the process of working with these people as having to go through labor pains all over again. The subject of spiritual pregnancy is quite encompassing throughout scripture.

Two Types of Spiritual Pregnancy

Two types of spiritual pregnancies take place in our lives. The first type is when we hear the Word of God and by faith accept Christ. In that moment, the rebirth of our spiritual man takes place, and if our hearts are good, fertile ground, we conceive and are "re-'gene'-erated." Spiritual regeneration is the first and most important pregnancy experience and birth that will ever happen. While this is true concerning our rebirth, it brings us to our second type of pregnancy.

A person has to conceive a ministry and be burdened with a passion for lost souls in order to reach out with God's Word to win others. That said, one can be pregnant with prison ministry, nursing home ministry, youth ministry, hurting women ministry, media ministry, or mentorship. The list goes on. Thus, spiritual pregnancy comes from spending intimate time with God and can take many forms.

Every business, company, work, or ministry has to be conceived and birthed, so there will be some illegitimate or bastard births as well. Just look at prostitution, drug dealing, and human trafficking. They are businesses that were conceived but are not legitimate. God did not father them. Just think of all the illegitimate churches, ministries, and religions that were conceived and are going on in the religious world.

Birth Control

It's important to note the necessity of family planning. I don't think we should just birth children naturally or spiritually without some type of preparation. However, the objective in ministry is to be fruitful and multiply. I think too many churches, ministries, and individual believers are on birth control. Think about it. Why are people on birth control? Is it primarily because of the inconvenience that would be caused by children we're not ready for? Perhaps they might interfere with our careers and ambitions?

What if Mary, the teenage mother of our Lord Jesus, had been on birth control and said, "No, I have other plans," or perhaps said, "I'm not ready to birth this ministry"? Thank God she allowed her life to be interrupted. A deeper look into Mary's situation from Luke 1:26–38 reveals more insight into spiritual pregnancy. The angel Gabriel greeted her, saying that she was blessed and highly favored among women. Although she was engaged to marry Joseph, he told her that she would conceive and birth the Son of God. Luke 1:35 says the Holy Ghost shall come upon her and the power of the highest shall overshadow her to cause this birth.

As we parallel our lives spiritually to Christ's being conceived in Mary under these circumstances, we can see that spiritual pregnancy alters our lives and directions drastically. But we're still highly favored and blessed among all people in the world. We can also see that we have an opportunity to conceive, birth, and present Christ to the world as Mary did. When we carry Christ in our hearts, not only do we carry a Savior, but we carry ministry, seed, purpose, destiny, and so much more. Christ within us wants to go about doing those things He came to do—that is, "seek and save the lost, make disciples ... not call the righteous but sinners to repentance," to preach the gospel to the poor, heal the brokenhearted, set captives free, and open blinded eyes (Luke 4:18).

These ministries are not birthed, manifested, or delivered to the world if we tie Jesus's hands. This brings us to another form of birth control—tubal ligation, also referred to as getting one's "tubes tied." Tubal ligation is when the physician ties the woman's fallopian tubes to block the eggs that are released from the ovaries from passing through the tubes. This blockage prevents the sperm from meeting and fertilizing any of the released eggs, thus preventing conception or pregnancy. Typically, for this procedure to take place a woman has to sign a consent form, allowing the gynecologist or surgeon, as well as the anesthesiologist and his or her staff, to put her to sleep and tie her tubes. This is considered sterilization, a permanent method of birth control.

Let's look at the spiritual application of tubal ligation. In Mark 7:1–13, Jesus talked to the Pharisees and scribes, declaring that they rejected the commandment of God and were, in essence, making the Word of God of no effect through their traditions. He said they were teaching and making into doctrine man-made commandments. In Acts 5:29, Peter and the other apostles said, "We ought to obey God rather than men." These passages show us what spiritual tubal ligation is and how to avoid it. Certain religious traditions, customs, man-made doctrines, denominations, governing boards, and organizations can nullify the effectiveness of God's Word.

As mentioned, tubal ligation requires a signed informed consent and that we trust the physician and staff. Spiritually, we join a church or ministry, submitting to that leadership after finding out about it. Sometimes, as with surgical procedures, we don't research as we should, and we trust what we've heard about a leader or ministry too easily. It's ultimately our responsibility, if we join that church or ministry, to know what they stand for, whether right or wrong.

Another part of the natural process involves the anesthesiologist putting you to sleep. While unconscious under general anesthesia, the brain doesn't respond to pain signals, and you're unable to feel pain. This would be equivalent to allowing leadership to cause you to be numb to what's going on around you. In a healthy sense, we should submit to true leadership and trust the direction it's going, but all too often, we allow leadership to silence our convictions. People are lost, hurting, starving, and dying all around us, but we don't feel the need to reach out because we're asleep, or anesthetized, trusting our leadership.

Remember the words of Jesus in Matthew 15:14. "If the blind lead the blind, they'll both fall into a ditch." Besides individual convictions and assignments, many of our churches, denominations, and pastors have been put to sleep. After a while, we're numb to much of what's going on in our communities and the world at large. Ephesians 5:14 says we're to wake up if we've been put to sleep, and arise from the dead so that Christ can shine His light on us.

Now, let's look at the actual procedure of tubal ligation. The surgeon or gynecologist goes into the abdomen, inserting instruments used to block off the tubes. The tubes may be burned shut by cauterization or be clamped off. Either way, the egg and sperm are not able to meet for reproduction.

Let's look at a couple of passages that can relate to tubal ligation. First Timothy 4:2 speaks of having our "conscience seared with a hot iron." The word "seared" is also translated as "cauterized" or "branded." I'll let the scholars fully exegete the text here, but I do like the similar terminology used when referring to the tubes being cauterized. Either way, whether false teachers or believers engaged in repetitive sin, something hinders one from living a fruitful Christian life. It blocks the effectiveness of God's Word or seed in our lives.

Another relevant passage is the parable of the sower (Matt. 13 and Mark 4). Jesus said the cares of this life, along with the deceitfulness of riches and the lust for other things, can choke the Word (seed or sperm) and cause it to be unfruitful (Mark 4:18). If we aren't careful, things can enter and tie our tubes. These things are the instruments man or the devil uses to hinder or block our spiritual pregnancy, just as with the instruments in the tubal ligation procedure.

For pregnancy to take place, there has to be ovulation. Ovulation is the release of the mature egg from the female's ovary. The sperm has to connect with the egg at the right time. If the tubes are tied, it may be the right time but the connection still can't be made spiritually. You're having intimacy with God, and the Word is moving within you but never quite making the connection to be able to reproduce—all because you have allowed man, the devil, or sin to tie your spiritual tubes. It's important to note that sometimes the procedure can be reversed, and I believe this would be through repentance. It may be that you need to find another progressive-minded ministry to join. And if you can't get another leader to undo what "man" has done to you, you may have to ask God. In Galatians 5, Paul speaks concerning the freedom we have in Christ and says we shouldn't be entangled again with the yoke of bondage or attempt to be justified by works of the law. Again, this sounds like getting our tubes tied, entangled, or yoked up in bondage, making Christ, who is the Word of God, of no effect (Gal. 5:4). Then Paul goes on to say, "Ye did run well; who did hinder you that ye should not obey the truth?" (Gal. 5:7). Man can tie your spiritual tubes through erroneous teaching.

Let's look at a few more methods of birth control. Barriers such as condoms, diaphragm, cervical caps, and sponges prevent the sperm from entering the cervix and getting to the egg. Again, you can enjoy intimacy, but there's something that's man-made preventing conception or pregnancy. Spiritually, are you enjoying the presence of God, the worship, teaching, preaching, singing, or even personal intimate time with God, yet you have a barrier or wall up, stopping the Word from causing your pregnancy? Or have you allowed man to implant something within you that hinders the Word?

The IUD, or intrauterine device, is a very popular

contraceptive method. A health care provider has to insert this device into the uterus. One type of IUD uses hormones, while the other uses copper. The copper damages the sperm's motility and hinders it from reaching the egg, which prevents fertilization. Remember the sperm represents the Word of God. As we look at this spiritually, we see the copper hindering the Word of God from causing fruitfulness. As an element, copper is needed in small amounts in the body for proper organ functioning, metabolism, and homeostasis. This equivocates to the proper functioning ministries operating harmoniously within the body of Christ. Copper is used to make pennies, and as the age-old saying goes, it takes pennies to make dollars—which is money. We need money in the right amount to carry out ministries, but used inappropriately, it can be a hindrance. The body has a way of regulating its use of copper. Spiritually, we, as the body of Christ, should be prayerful in our use of the money that comes in. If we allow man to insert his teachings or copper-coated IUD within our spiritual uterus, we make way for money to be used inappropriately or go to the wrong place, hindering the motility of the Word and altogether preventing conception.

Paul warns in 1 Timothy 6 concerning the improper use and desire of money in the Christian life. In 1 Timothy 6:5, he says that some "suppose that godliness is a means of financial gain," with the New Living Translation stating, "These people always cause trouble. Their minds are corrupt, and have turned their backs on the truth. To them, a show of godliness is just a way to become wealthy." First Timothy 6:10 talks about the "love of money" being what causes some to stray from the faith in greediness, piercing themselves with many sorrows. In verses 17–19, Paul warns the rich to do good and be rich in good works, always ready to give or spread the copper. Ecclesiastes 11:1–2 says, "Cast your bread upon the waters ... give a serving to seven, and also to eight." Don't just keep it to yourself. Finally, the rich young ruler in Mark 10 didn't have his copper in the right place when Jesus told him to go sell all he had and give to the poor in order to have treasure in heaven. In Mark 10:23–24, Jesus warned that it was hard for those who have riches or to trust in them to enter the kingdom of God. This was another case of the copper hindering the birthing of souls or fruitful Christianity. So repent, remove your spiritual IUD, and be fruitful in the kingdom of God. Prayerfully put the copper where it's needed.

The final method of birth control I'll touch on is the rhythm method. As stated, the only time that pregnancy can take place is when the female ovulates. I believe this is God's original design. The ovulation period usually occurs around the halfway point of a twenty-eight-day cycle. If we don't move intimately with God at this time, pregnancy won't happen. Ecclesiastes 3 says that there's a season and time for every purpose under heaven. We shouldn't plan to not be ready when God wants to fertilize our egg. This is something we can see in Ecclesiastes 11:5 and also in John 3:8, when Jesus is talking to Nicodemus concerning spiritual rebirth. He says the wind blows where it wishes, but you can tell where it's coming from or going to go. Stop holding back while God is moving in your life.

Infertility

In biblical times, primarily in the Old Testament, it was a shame for a woman to be barren, or infertile. Often, God would miraculously bless such women to bear children (e.g., Sarah, Rachel, Hannah, and Samson's mother). As always, we look at the natural and then the spiritual. Since physical childbirth is symbolic of the spiritual rebirthing of souls into the kingdom of

God or the birthing of our ministries, we must find out what God is saying to us through infertility.

In our day and culture, it's not a shame for a woman to be unable to have children, but I do think it's somewhat of a shame if we can't bear fruit spiritually. John 15 says God desires us to bear much fruit, and if we don't, we'll be cut off and burned. This is scary!

According to the CDC, Mayo Clinic, and NIH, infertility is the inability to get pregnant despite trying for one year. This includes if a woman is able get pregnant but keeps having miscarriages or stillbirths. It's also considered a disease or abnormality of the reproductive system. Thus, if we can't get pregnant spiritually or carry the pregnancy full term with a live delivery, we must have a spiritual disease, disorder, or some type of abnormality.

Although our primary focus in this chapter is our being female, as the body of Christ, and God being the male depositing the sperm into us causing pregnancy, we also see the church as male because Christ is the head of His body. This is also supported by the fact that Christ, in 1 Corinthians 15, is called the last Adam. In Genesis 2, God put Adam to sleep and pulled Eve from inside. Thus, the female was inside the male, just as we are the bride of Christ inside of Him. There's yet another perspective: that in Christ, there's neither male nor female. Don't get hung up on the gender thing or put God in a box. At times we are the female being impregnated by God to birth ministry, and at other times we operate as the male body of Christ, spreading the seed/sperm/Word of God to impregnate others, whether the lost or those already saved.

Male Infertility

Infertility in the male can be caused by a low sperm count. In other words, if we don't have much Word in us, we're less likely to impregnate anyone. Another cause is lack of desire. As the male, you're less likely to have sex, erection, or ejaculate if you don't have much desire. Spiritually, there definitely has to be excitement and intensity in order to adequately propel the Word out there to the world.

If the libido (sex drive) is low, it usually affects the intimacy in relationships, all resulting in a decreased chance of pregnancy. That said, if we're not hungry for God, His kingdom, and righteousness, we're less likely to win souls, reproduce, or become pregnant with ministry.

Factors Affecting the Sex Drive

On the physical side, various factors can affect the sex drive, such as stress, low testosterone levels, illness, or medications. You can look at what Jesus said in Mark 4 concerning "the cares of this life" choking out the Word, causing it to become unfruitful in our lives. So often, we get involved with things that distract us, hindering our intimacy with God.

One of those things can be infidelity. Unfaithfulness or cheating on God can interfere with the intimacy in a relationship but can also be an indication that a partner's sexual desires are no longer satisfied in the relationship. In Revelation 2, Jesus warns the church of Ephesus about leaving their first love. He told them to repent and get back to what they used to do in the relationship to keep the fire burning. Technically, one can engage in sexual activity without having the desire for it, so I'm sure this happens quite often spiritually—going through the motions while doing the works of God but with no real passion for it. This is also evident in Revelation 3 concerning the Sardis church. Jesus said they had a name, that they were alive, but were really a dead or impotent church.

What about the Laodicean church that was neither hot nor cold? This church was totally complacent in its relationship with God. They forgot who put food on the table and clothes on their backs and thought they had it going on. But Jesus was on the outside looking in, knocking at the door of their hearts, desiring to come in and have intimate fellowship with them. It's a sad thing to think that your partner is satisfied sexually in a relationship just because you're getting what *you* want. Also, we may even take our mate for granted the longer we're together. In each case, Jesus is saying "repent," and let's come back together intimately so that we can be fruitful.

As we age, we become less fertile, whether the cause is low testosterone levels, decreased sex drive, or increased health problems. I think the message here is clear: We must remember our Creator in the days of our youth while the evil days come not, and we say, I have no pleasure in them (Eccles. 12:1). Often, as we age spiritually, the drive decreases. The drive to witness or even spend intimate time with God may decrease. The drive to birth new ministries may be low.

While the capacity to reproduce is decreased as the female approaches menopause physically, the same can be said spiritually. After age thirty-five, the female is a lot less fertile. Sarah had a child, Isaac, at age ninety, but this was considered a miracle. All this shows us what God can do if only we have faith in Him. Remember—we act as male or female in the spirit.

As the female, our capacity to birth new ministries decreases as we age. But as the male, our sperm count stays up much longer than the egg total of the female. To me, this is saying that we can pass the torch or mantle, impregnating the younger generation with the seed or sperm of the Word, even in our older years. We are dreaming dreams as we age while the young are being impregnated with new vision (Joel 2).

Female Infertility

Several things increase a woman's risk of infertility. Age is a major cause of infertility in women (according to the CDC). A woman's chances of having a baby decrease rapidly every year after age thirty. Many women are waiting longer to have babies. Whether waiting to "get it all together" or because of career goals or financial reasons, the older we get, the more our windows of opportunity decrease. Irregular menstrual periods could be a cause. The female has to ovulate to get pregnant, and if she's having very irregular periods, it's often a sign that she's not ovulating. Spiritually, if someone is irregular, inconsistent, undependable, or unfaithful when it comes to ministry or the things of God, they are less likely to be fruitful as a Christian.

On average, the normal menstrual cycle is twenty-eight days long. Day one is considered to be the first day of "full flow." Spiritually, the blood of Jesus must fully flow consistently in our lives and ministries for spiritual pregnancy to be possible. Trusting in His sacrifice, in which He shed His blood, is the only reason we have a chance to reproduce. If we consistently omit the blood from our songs, sermons, and ministries, we are less likely to be productive, as God intended.

Rape

I'm discussing rape because pregnancy occasionally occurs from rape, but here, it's only for a spiritual message that I bring up such a sensitive subject. My primary source for information on rape is RAINN (Rape, Abuse, Incest National Network), the largest antisexual violence organization in the United States. Although this source is not intended for legal advice, you can gain some insightful information on the subject.

Rape is sometimes referred to as sexual assault, even though all sexual assault is not considered rape. No matter the source, it all involves force and sexual activity without consent. Force can be physical, emotional, psychological, or any other form of threat to get a victim to give in. So much of this occurs in ministry. Leaders or even fellow church members force themselves on others to gain pleasure from them.

The majority of perpetrators are someone known to the victim. Acquaintance or date rape may occur because it's someone you come to know and trust spiritually, and they later abuse you. They may flirt with you spiritually, telling you all the great things God has for you, while all along wanting to get inside your clothes to get your wallet. They may threaten you by the misuse of their spiritual authority. Just as your employer may threaten you with your potential firing if you don't sleep with him or her, the same goes on spiritually. A minister, pastor, or prophet you trust may threaten your financial well-being if you don't give to their offering for personal gain. "You're going to be cursed in your finances," or "Bad things are going to happen to you" if you don't give in and do what they say or want.

Also, Satan is the ultimate rapist. Just as he flirted with Eve in the garden in Genesis 3, he flirted with the Messiah in Matthew 4, offering Him all the kingdoms of the world if only Jesus would bow down and worship him. He was using his power as the "god of this world" to get adoration for his own selfish pleasure (2 Cor. 4:4; Eph. 2:2).

So often the young, vulnerable female or children under twelve are the victims of sexual assault. I relate this to new or baby Christians as ones who are often raped or molested by the ones they trust or look up to in ministry. This is one reason that we have to be more watchful and protective of the new converts, whether it's from the secular, worldly lusts, schemes, false religions, or leaders and professing Christians within our own Christian fellowships. There are dangerous predators and perpetrators everywhere, so always be alert and prayerful.

Avoid Dangerous Situations

Here are a few ways to help reduce the risk of spiritual rape:

1. *Always be aware of your surroundings.* First Peter 5:8 says that we should be sober and vigilant because the devil is going around as a roaring lion, looking for someone to devour. He wants to blitz rape you as he did Job, suddenly and brutally (Job 1–2). Scriptures also tell us to know those who labor among you because they may have to help you out of a bad situation.
2. *Avoid being isolated.* Even when doing the work of the Lord, Jesus sent His disciples out two by two, in Luke 10. It's good to have a prayer partner or witnessing partner. Satan, that ol' wolf, loves to get sheep off to themselves, isolated from the rest of the flock. The parking-lot prophets love to get you off by yourself and seduce you for their own pleasure. They won't try to minister to you around your other true, seasoned leaders or fellow believers.
3. *Walk with purpose.* If you don't know where you're going, you're more of a target for the spiritual predator. Even if you haven't discovered your purpose, walk and work for God confidently, blooming where you're planted.

4. *Try not to get overloaded.* Just as you appear more vulnerable with bags and packages in the physical sense, the same is true spiritually. If you're stressed out, have a lot of baggage in your life, or you're simply trying to do too much, the predator sees an opportunity to overtake you. Therefore, cast all your cares upon Christ because He cares for you (1 Pet. 5:7). Also, in Matthew 11:28, Jesus says to come to Him, all who labor and are heavy laden, and He'll give you rest. Sometimes we need to just rest at His feet.

5. *Keep your cell phone charged and with you, and have cab fare to get back home.* So often we get abused or taken advantage of when we're out doing ministry, whether preaching or teaching or giving concerts or conferences. Our gifts may be attractive to some people who only want to get a thrill from us. Jesus said we should not give that which is holy to the dogs or cast our pearls before the swine, lest they turn and trample on us (Matt. 7:6).

You could find yourself in some compromising position, so you must always have your spiritual cell phone with you and charged to be able to call your Savior or Christian brother or sister to come get you. Don't go anywhere that you can't get back home, depending on the person or people who booked you. It's like going on a date with someone, and you don't give the person what he or she wants. He or she may put you out or have you walk back home.

All in all, don't go on dates with the devil if you don't want to get into compromising positions. He's a date-raping sexual predator, always looking to take advantage of naïve, trusting, unsuspecting people. He uses the attractive things of this secular world to lure us into dangerous places and then forces himself on us. You could become pregnant with something that could be very costly in the long run.

False Pregnancy

The clinical term for false pregnancy is *pseudocyesis*. Even though the causes are not fully understood, a female believes she is pregnant while actually exhibiting signs and symptoms of pregnancy. Even experienced practitioners can be baffled because the symptoms of pseudocyesis mimic true pregnancy so well. Although psychological issues are usually involved, those of pseudocyesis are different from the delusions of people with psychotic disorders, such as schizophrenia. This condition is also different from someone who is pretending to be pregnant for other reasons. The person with a false pregnancy may be exhibiting signals because she has had miscarriages or is infertile and has an intense desire to become pregnant. She may have a swollen abdomen and sensation of fetal movement, but there's no baby inside; she's tested negative.

As we look in the world of ministry, we'll often observe people with spiritual psychosis as well, thinking they are God's chosen apostles or prophets, with no visible evidence or affirmation. In Matthew 3, John the Baptist warned certain religious leaders to bring him some fruit, or evidence, proving that they were who they said they were. In other words, there *are* those who are deceitful workers and, as Paul called them, "false apostles or ministers" (2 Cor. 11:13). The spiritually psychotic are delusional with the belief but no evidence to back up their claim.

Those with a false spiritual pregnancy really believe that they are pregnant, but unlike the psychotic, they exhibit signs mimicking true pregnancy. They are infertile or have had multiple spiritual miscarriages because of certain occurrences in the past but have a really intense desire to be pregnant and show signs and symptoms. Maybe you have failed in an attempt to get your ministry off the ground on multiple occasions and really want to succeed at it this time. If this is the case, and you really believe you are pregnant with a particular ministry, let your spiritual leader run a pregnancy test on you.

In the case of pseudocyesis, the brain may be misinterpreting a few signs as pregnancy that trigger a release of certain hormones, actually leading to pregnancy symptoms. Sometimes certain things happen in our lives, or we read the Bible and misinterpret these signals as pregnancy. Perhaps we're in an awesome church service or conference and hear certain things we interpret as a sign of our time or season.

Finally, there are researchers who think that childhood sexual abuse, relationship problems, poverty, and lack of education could be various contributing factors in triggering a false pregnancy. Relating this spiritually, maybe you were abused early in your spiritual life by someone you looked up to and trusted. It could be that you were in financial need and thought that your starting a church could be your way out. Maybe you just couldn't get along with others in a shared ministry and thought that if you started your own, it would be a good thing and would prevent other problems. It could be a case of a lack of education or scriptural knowledge that causes you to believe you're pregnant. Any of the abovementioned could be playing a role in the belief of pregnancy and contributing to signs and symptoms of it. While it's true that some leaders, just like seasoned practitioners, can "miss it" or even want to hold you back, it may be for you to continue to work in that ministry. You may think somebody is limiting you, but that does not necessarily mean it is time to leave. It may be time for you to remain and learn to work through the challenge or work through adversity. Other times, you may have to get a second opinion.

Preparing for Pregnancy

We all have a calling on our lives to fulfill the great commission of going all over the world, spreading the gospel and reaching people for Christ. We're to help prepare people to do the same thing by making disciples.

Intimacy and Ovulation

As mentioned earlier, spiritual pregnancy is when we spend intimate time with God, conceive, and give birth to our personal method or ministry. There's a time during the month when a mature female can become pregnant, which is during ovulation. This is what God is saying to us in several passages of scripture, but especially in Ecclesiastes 3, concerning a season for everything and a time for every purpose. Genesis 8 speaks about seedtime and harvest always being while the earth exists. Thus, there's a time and season for you to become pregnant and birth your ministry or purpose. If you're not intimately involved, spiritually, don't expect to become pregnant with purpose, and if you fail to be intimate with God and the things of God, you may miss your season.

Since ovulation is the only time during the cycle a female who wants to have a baby can become pregnant, she must be sexually active at that time. Some women are regular, others are not, which may be due to stress, exercising, hard work, or other factors. This is also true spiritually. Martha was so busy "working" for Jesus that she was stressed out, while her sister, Mary, was intimately at His feet, allowing Him to pour into her (Luke 10:38–42). Truly, the words Christ speaks are spirit and life (John 6:63), impregnating the hearers. While we need both the servitude of Martha and the intimate fellowship of Mary with our Lord, we must work to have a proper balance. We must always seek God's kingdom first.

Perhaps Mary had the ingredients to help cause the birthing of the miracle that raised her brother, Lazarus, from the dead. In John 11, Jesus was deeply moved when she fell at His feet in tears and asked Mary where they had laid Lazarus. In a sense, Christ went into labor, and the miracle of resurrection was birthed. Martha was there as well, but she was trying to make it happen, while Mary just worshipped and let it happen.

Intimacy, Attraction, and Excitement

In a good relationship, there has to be intimacy. It involves a close and open relationship, making the other person feel that he or she is the most important person in the world. Intimacy means removing layers of things you are covered with to be naked without shame before your partner. It's making yourself vulnerable and trusting that your partner won't hurt you, even though you expose your emotional or physical flaws to him or her.

If only we would be open and honest with our Lord and Savior, trusting that He would never hurt us; we would be so much closer. He says in Hebrew 4 that we're naked before Him anyway, and He was touched with similar feelings and infirmities as we are. God knows all the baggage we have in our lives but loves us just the same. Sin does cause scandal and shame, as it did with Adam and Eve in Genesis 3 after they had fallen. But if you'll notice, in Genesis 2 before they sinned, they were both naked and not ashamed. God was ready for his regular intimate fellowship, but after sinning, they were embarrassed, paranoid, and now hiding. The good news is that Christ, the last Adam, came to reconcile our relationship and restore the intimacy. Don't be ashamed to show Him your wounds and scars, because He showed us His openly on the cross.

There needs to be an attraction in the relationship leading to healthy sexual intimacy. Just as you dress a certain way and put on certain fragrances to create a romantic atmosphere, the same applies to our Christ relationship. God is attracted to lingerie of repentance, humility, and brokenness, as David suggested in Psalm 51. He's really drawn in by worship from a sincere, pure heart. It creates an irresistible fragrance up to God when we offer ourselves as living sacrifices to God through Christ (2 Cor. 2:14–15; Eph. 5:2; Gen. 8:20–21). Also, Luke 7 speaks of the sinful woman who attracted Christ with her tears and brokenness but also brought an alabaster jar of expensive perfume to anoint Him. She washed His feet with her tears and dried them with her hair. This was awesome intimacy. Spiritually, she was ready to get pregnant.

Now that we've covered attraction, we've set the stage for excitement. Excitement, here, means sexual arousal or being turned on. Sin turns God off, just as a dirty partner with a terrible body odor turns you off, even more so when that partner has been unfaithful to you and has caught an STD, causing him or her to smell. It would be especially bad to have soap and water (even antibiotics for your infection) available but refuse to use them and still expect your partner to be turned on. It's an altogether different story if both you and your partner are dirty and smelling from the same filth. Neither of you can tell—or smell—the difference. Otherwise, you would say, "Hold on a minute; let's talk."

This is exactly what God is saying in Isaiah 1:18, when He said, "Come now and let us reason together, ... though your sins are as scarlet" or "red as crimson," He'll wash us "as white as snow." In this case, God will give you a bath in lamb's blood, and then you'll be ready for an exciting time of refreshing from the presence of the Lord. You'll be overshadowed by the Holy

Spirit as Mary was and conceive a holy thing. If you didn't get pregnant this time around, don't worry, because ovulation will happen again, just as seasons change. Just be ready, consistent, and remain intimately involved, and your time will come.

Signs and Symptoms of Pregnancy

Signs and symptoms occurring during pregnancy can be subjective, objective, or diagnostic. Subjective symptoms are those experienced by the female and reported but could also be caused by other conditions. Objective symptoms are those observed or noticed by an examiner. Diagnostic changes are positive and offer conclusive proof of pregnancy. I'm only mentioning some of these that occur throughout the different trimesters.

First Trimester

1. *Amenorrhea.* This is when a woman misses her period, which is usually the first sign of pregnancy in a healthy woman. It's fitting that the "blood" would be the first indicator of pregnancy in the spirit also. Rather than the blood being released from the body monthly, as it normally would, it's now going from the mother to the baby. So in your ministry that you're carrying, know that the blood of Christ is vital for it to survive.
2. *Nausea and vomiting.* This often occurs in the morning and is usually in the first trimester. This is my personal opinion, but I believe it's nature's or God's way of alerting and preventing a woman from eating or drinking anything that would be harmful to her developing infant. Most birth defects occur during the first trimester, which is the most crucial time of development of the fetus's organs and

systems. When God impregnates you, you must take great care in guarding your unborn ministry. If you become unable to stomach some of what others are teaching, maybe it's a sign that you're pregnant. It may be good food but not for you at the time. Seek and acknowledge God early in the morning before leaving the house in order to settle your stomach and to help you deal with your daily discomforts. Commune with God early, eating His daily bread for your pregnancy, and you won't have look for someone to make you feel like what you're carrying is of God. Your stomach will already be settled, and you won't have to vomit a bunch of negativity from other people who don't believe in you.

3. *Excessive fatigue.* Your body is now adjusting to carrying another life, which can be very taxing early on. When God places the burden of carrying a new ministry within you, the fatigue you're now experiencing is saying, "Slow down," and care for what's been imparted in you.

4. *Urinary frequency.* Something growing inside of you is now pressuring your bladder and causing frequent urination. If urination is removing waste and toxins from the body while emptying the bladder, then you understand that with spiritual pregnancy there's an increased pressure to repent frequently and remove things from your life while carrying a new ministry. In other words, you want things to be right when you birth your new ministry, so you leave your gift at the altar and go to be reconciled with your brother. Also, you go to God frequently, asking Him to search you and remove anything that could hinder or hurt your baby that's developing within you.

5. *Breast swelling and tenderness.* Hormonal changes cause the breasts to enlarge, preparing for breastfeeding.

This enlargement and increased sensitivity is suggestive of an increase in your capacity to nourish. You're no longer living your Christian life for yourself but are now burdened as well as blessed with the ability to be a blessing. Sometimes you have to painfully search for ways to nourish or connect with your ministry. The pain and sensitivity in your breast area is letting you know that the preparation to nourish others can be quite uncomfortable. This is an early sign, telling you to get ready by studying to show yourself approved by God. There will be times that you'll be rejected while wanting more for people than they want for themselves. Also, breastfeeding will be a time of bonding for you and your ministry.

The tenderness is an early sign that's sensitizing you to prepare yourself for what's ahead. Nobody will love and nurture your ministry like you will. Others may put a bottle in the baby's mouth, but you'll actually be bonding more intimately because of the spiritual breastfeeding you'll do.

Second Trimester

1. *Body aches.* While early symptoms like fatigue and morning sickness may be subsiding here, other discomforts, like abdominal, back, and groin pain, are starting. These pains are to be expected because something is growing inside of you. As it grows, it's causing you to grow with it, but it's changing your body rapidly. These are the pains of preparation and increasing capacity to do ministry.
2. *Stretch marks.* These marks usually occur on your abdomen, breasts, and other areas. This rapid growth is stretching the skin beyond what it's used to. When God impregnates

you, He's placing something in you that's going to grow and stretch you beyond your comfort zone. It's likely that it will leave "stretch marks" forever, reminding you of your potential. If He did it once, He can do it again.

3. *Weight gain.* The baby is now growing and extending your abdomen. In other words, you're starting to show. It's becoming obvious to others that you're carrying something. You're getting bigger and are beginning to be noticed in your church, ministry, and the world.

4. *Fetal movement—quickening.* This is when the mother first feels or perceives the baby is moving or kicking inside. This happened when Elizabeth felt the baby "leap" in her womb when she came in contact with Mary, who was carrying Jesus at the time (Luke 1). We walk by faith, but there are times when God will let you feel what He's placed inside of you. Sometimes you may have to do as Mary did when she went to Elizabeth, who is someone else that God had caused to become pregnant in a miraculous way. Elizabeth's baby leaped when coming in contact with pregnant Mary. It's a sign that the presence of someone carrying Jesus can reassure you and can cause *your* baby to leap for joy. Success breeds success, iron sharpens iron, and being around productive people can bring to life what's inside you. I've had great ideas within me for years but they didn't come alive until I got around people who were already doing what I was dreaming about. They made my baby leap.

Third Trimester

1. *Body achiness.* As a baby grows, the pains and discomfort increase, such as round ligament and back pain. The

pull on your center of gravity may cause your back to ache. The weight of ministry is now causing an increased demand on you.

2. *Breast leaking.* You're getting prepared to nurse this developing baby. I remember when I first accepted my call to preach the gospel. I would often say that I was anointed to preach because it was so strong within that it was bursting out of me—or rather, "leaking" out. I couldn't help but tell people about the good news of Christ. I was warming up before actually giving birth to the ministry and work that God had for me.

3. *Trouble sleeping.* This can happen anytime during the pregnancy because of the emotional stress and the body's adjusting to something growing. Also, late in the pregnancy, it's like trying to sleep with a big watermelon in your belly. Birthing a new ministry or church will cause you to lose sleep at times. While Moses was carrying the children of Israel, they caused him to become restless (Num. 11:10–15; Deut. 1:9). Even the apostle Paul was burdened with the care of the churches (2 Cor. 11:28). In Acts 20:31, Paul says that with many tears he warned the people "night and day." A true leader will lose sleep at times because of the love and care he or she has for God's people.

4. *Fatigue.* As the baby gets bigger, the demand on you is greater than ever, resulting in greater fatigue. One time, Moses got to the point of saying that the burden was too much for him to bear. During this time, you may feel the stress of what you're carrying wearing you out, but you're now closer than you've ever been to your due date. Don't give up. Keep pressing on.

5. *Braxton-Hicks contractions.* These are irregular contractions that may occur throughout the pregnancy. They're generally painless but get more uncomfortable toward the end of pregnancy. They can be confused with true labor contractions and are sometimes referred to as "false labor." It may feel like true labor, but you're not dilating. These are practice labor contractions getting you ready for true labor. Also, they circulate blood through the placenta. Spiritually, we'll go through much discomfort before birthing a new ministry. During this phase, it's irregular, but you just have to keep working through your discomfort, and it will subside. Also, keep in mind that these "practice contractions" are helping circulate blood through the placenta. Your discomfort is blessing your baby by increasing the blood circulation there. The discomfort of the cross of Christ, with the blood He shed, must always be applied to what you're doing in ministry. Braxton-Hicks contractions are getting you ready for the labor that's up ahead.

   These contractions can be confused with the true labor contractions. Seasoned practitioners may have trouble discerning the difference between false labor contractions and true labor. There are a few major differences that I'll mention later while discussing true labor, but my major focus here is the cervix not dilating. During true labor, the cervix dilates for the baby to come out, but with false labor, there's no dilation. In other words, when it's your time, God will open the door for your ministry to come forth. You don't have to force the issue or try to make it happen. Don't be fooled by the inconsistent, moderate discomfort of false labor. This is similar to what God asked Jeremiah in Jeremiah 12:5. He asked that if Jeremiah was worn out from running with people on foot, how would he deal with the horses when they came? So I also ask you: if you can't deal with the discomfort of false labor contractions, how will you survive when the true birth pains of ministry come?

Pregnancy Risks

Numerous complications and risks can occur during pregnancy, such as gestational diabetes, preeclampsia, miscarriage, hypertension, bleeding, preterm labor, and many more. I'll touch briefly on a few that I found most intriguing.

A "miscarriage" is the lay term for "spontaneous abortion." It's when the pregnancy ends on its own within the first twenty weeks. After twenty weeks it's considered a "stillbirth." Most sources I found stated that 10–20 percent of known pregnancies end in miscarriage, with the majority ending in the first trimester. There are several possible causes of miscarriage, but most probably occur when the baby has fatal genetic problems, which may or may not be related to the parent. We were taught that it was nature's way of preventing an unhealthy baby from being born. Other possible causes include infection, medical conditions, hormonal issues, or a certain physical problem in the mother.

Spiritually, it's easy to understand how miscarriages can occur if something is wrong with the person carrying the baby or ministry. If you have a spiritual infection (sin) in your life, or you have been damaged from *past* sins, it's understandable that you can have a miscarriage. If your life is out of balance spiritually because you have spiritual diabetes or other issues, it would not be too shocking if you miscarried in this case either. But what about the fatal genetic problems that may be the cause but are unrelated to the mother? (By the way, I don't believe in the evolutionary process of natural selection as being the cause of miscarriage. I believe life is created by God.)

In a miscarriage, the primary thing I look at is that the pregnancy ended on its own. Spiritually, I think this occurs when you want to take people where they aren't ready or willing to go, just as Moses attempted to lead the Hebrew children out of Egypt to that blessed Promised Land, but most spontaneously aborted or miscarried in the wilderness. It's what Jesus experienced in Nazareth, where Matthew 13 and Mark 6 state that He could "do no miracles" or "mighty work there." There was nothing wrong with Jesus, so it was the people who miscarried or spontaneously aborted what He was trying to do for them. The same could be the case with you. Just because what you were carrying aborted spontaneously doesn't always mean that something was wrong with you.

If a spiritual genetic problem caused the miscarriage, it means there are errors or faulty information within the person or people being miscarried. In other words, the way people perceive Christ, you, or themselves could be what's hindering them from being carried full term. We often want more for people than they want for themselves, or we believe that they are capable of accomplishing more than they believe they can. So just go get pregnant again. Pray about it and start another ministry, business, or work for God.

As Paul stated in Philippians 1:6, "That He which hath begun a good work in you will perform it" or complete it. Make sure that you are healthy enough to carry a child or ministry. Check yourself for sin or spiritual imbalances that could cause you to miscarry. If you're bleeding or spotting, just rest because it may be a sign that you're overdoing things.

There are several types of miscarriages and stages, such as inevitable, complete, missed, and septic, but I only discussed the general term.

Spontaneous abortion is involuntary, but the other type of

abortion is not a complication; rather, it's a voluntary or elective abortion. To terminate a pregnancy because you're not ready to be a mother is similar to birth control, except the child has already been conceived. If God impregnates you, spiritually, please don't terminate it because it is an inconvenience to you.

Think about Mary, who was interrupted to carry our Savior. It may have been an inconvenience, but she agreed and carried the baby full term. Don't let it be for financial reasons either, because if God is the Father, He'll always provide for His own. However, if you've been impregnated by Satan, you definitely need to abort that pregnancy because you're getting ready to birth something that's illegitimate.

Stillbirths

After twenty weeks of pregnancy, the spontaneous termination of the pregnancy is considered a stillbirth. It's similar to a miscarriage, but the unborn child is further along in the pregnancy. How often have you seen people or a church with great plans for something new, but it never actually came to fruition? In theory, it was a great idea. They had capable people, but it was a bust. The idea was delivered, whether on time or before time, but it never came to life. A stillbirth may have all the physical features and body systems in place, but nothing is functioning.

As with miscarriages, there are several possible causes of stillbirths, including untreated infection, placental damage, genetic conditions, preterm labor, hypertension, eclampsia, drug use, obesity, and more. Listed are a few in detail:

1. *Preterm labor.* It's always a risk if the baby is coming too early because there is a due date for a reason. The Bible speaks of there being a time and season for everything. If

you try to give birth to your baby or ministry too soon, it could harm or destroy your work. You saw through an ultrasound that it appeared to be growing normally and should function, but you, people, or the devil tried to make it happen before it was time.

2. *Placental problems.* This involves problems such as placental abruption, where the placenta detaches or separates from the uterus. The placenta is what nourishes the baby with food and oxygen. If you disconnect yourself or allow the devil to cause you to stop nourishing your dream or vision, you could be setting yourself up for a stillbirth. It may die inside of you. Don't let people discourage you. Keep pouring into that with which God has impregnated you.

3. *Infection.* When left untreated, infection can harm or even cause the death of your baby. Sin is an infection that can hurt or kill your ministry before it even gets started. God will treat it if you give it to Him.

4. *Hypertension. Hyper* means too much *tension*, and added tension, stress, or pressure within is not good for you. It's also dangerous to your baby. This is true both physically and spiritually. It can decrease the blood flow to the placenta, which can deprive the baby of nutrients and oxygen. Therefore, keep the pressure down, allowing the peace of God to rule in your life. You must always remember to keep the blood of Christ flowing to your unborn ministry, dream, or vision.

Breech Presentation

The baby usually delivers presenting the head first, but if the buttocks or feet come first, it's called a breech presentation. This means the baby is not coming out in the proper order. There's more risk of the baby dying, being injured, or having other birth defects; there's also a danger to the mother.

There are three types of breech presentations: frank, complete, and footling breech. With the first two types, the buttocks is positioned near the cervix to present first. The footling breech is when one or both feet present first. Spiritually, the head should come out first, which suggests thought, planning, and order to your ministry. If the buttocks presents first, this is saying that the backside is first. The buttocks is often called your "backside." You may be doing things in a backward manner with your ministry. When your baby's foot or feet present first, it's suggestive of you attempting to get ahead of yourself with your dream, vision, or ministry. Sometimes you simply have to go through the ranks in order to get your ministry to where it should be. God has an order that needs to be maintained; otherwise, you may risk death, defect, or deformity to your new ministry.

In approaching a breech presentation, an experienced practitioner may be able to reposition the baby inside you through a procedure known as *version*. The manipulation of the baby could be by external or internal version, but external cephalic is the most common. Sometimes we have to allow our spiritual leader to redirect what we're trying to get done. Even though God has put this ministry in you, sometimes you need a seasoned person or people to help bring it out properly through advice or mentorship. Our pride will often have us saying, "I know what God has placed inside me, and this is my ministry." We may even think that others are trying to control us or hold us back, and that can be the case at times, but for the most part, there are greater risks to us and our ministry if we try to do it alone. Ephesians 4 tells us that God made us dependent on each other.

Cesarean Section (C-Section)

Some women may need to deliver through a cesarean section (also called C-section), which is delivery of the baby by a surgical procedure through an incision. Some practitioners would never attempt to deliver a breech birth vaginally because of the risk to the fetus. This is suggestive of your ministry's having complications and your needing to be cut in a different way from the normal in order to bring it out. You definitely need help if you require a C-section for delivery, and God has people who can help you.

There are other reasons that your practitioner may recommend a C-section, including stalled labor, being past due, carrying multiples, health concerns, or the baby's head being too large. When the baby's head is too large to pass through the birth canal, it's called cephalopelvic disproportion (CPD). Sometimes, what you're carrying is too big to come out the normal way. Or you may be past due for some reason and require an unusual means, or cut, to birth your vision. You may need a "spiritual C-section," but ultimately, God will use people to help bring it forth.

Several people in scripture probably had C-sections to birth their visions or dreams. One example would be Joseph. Although God had given him a great vision, he was sold into slavery (Genesis 37–50). Even though it was all a part of God's master plan, foreshadowing the life of Christ, there are elements that could be related to the spiritual C-section message. While in prison, Joseph was interpreting dreams and asked the butler to remember him when he got blessed by putting in a good word to Pharaoh for him. The butler forgot all about Joseph, but God had a due date for him, regardless of his being imprisoned. God had a C-section planned (for two years later) in order to cut out what Joseph had inside. Instead of the normal cut to birth his dream, others told lies about him and put him in prison in Egypt. God brought the dream to pass through a different means than what he was expecting.

True Labor

When a woman enters labor, it's an unknown area in her life. While this is especially true with the first experience, each experience is unique because you don't know how things will play out. You could require a C-section or experience complications that are not expected. Also, numerous factors can influence the reaction to the physical as well as emotional stress of labor. The same is true when birthing a new ministry. It's an unknown world where there's so much to fear. You don't know whether or not you can deal with the pains of birthing this new ministry, even though the inevitable is now imminent. You wonder if you'll have a good enough support system to assist in implementing your new vision. Either way, it's too late to back out. Labor is about to start.

Premonitory Signs of Labor

Before true labor begins, certain warning signs occur, signaling its imminent onset.

1. *Lightening.* This is the activity caused by the baby moving down into the pelvic inlet (engagement). The woman can breathe better with the pressure being off the diaphragm, but now there's increased pressure in the pelvic area, causing leg pain, cramps, and other discomforts.

    Now that your ministry is being thrust into position, knocking at the door to be birthed, there's more pressure on you or urgency to get it done. You may have relief in one area but increased pressure in another. Either way, you're closer than you've been to your due date, and the pressure is not going to go away until you birth what God has put inside you.

2. *Braxton-Hicks contractions.* As discussed earlier, these irregular contractions can occur throughout the pregnancy but are now becoming more uncomfortable. Some women may feel a "drawing" in the belly. If it gets so uncomfortable to where she thinks, "This is it," it's often called false labor. She may be confused, frustrated, and even embarrassed while going back and forth to the hospital, only to be sent away each time after being told, "Not yet."

   There may come a time when you think or truly believe that it's your time to give birth, but the door is not opening yet. It can be frustrating spiritually or even embarrassing because you thought you knew God well enough to know when it was time. You may have told people and made preparations, only to find out that it was not the time. It was false labor. But it's okay; people with great ministries have admitted to missing their due date and moving prematurely. Great football coaches have "missed it" with one team but took another to win the Super Bowl. How many times did Thomas Edison or the Wright brothers miss it before they actually birthed their visions? Just take the embarrassment as a sign that you're about to go into true labor and deliver.

3. *Bloody show.* This is the result of cervical secretions that accumulate in the cervical canal throughout the pregnancy to form a mucus plug that is expelled and results in a small amount of blood loss. This blood loss is pinkish and called "bloody show." It usually signals that true labor is imminent and delivery is soon to come, usually within twenty-four to forty-eight hours. This sounds very much like what happened at Calvary, a "bloody show" that led to our spiritual birth. The missed period (blood) is generally the first sign a woman notices, indicating that

she's pregnant. Bloody show (blood) is a major sign that she's about to go into labor before delivery.

4. *Water breaking.* This is also known as rupture of membranes. The baby is surrounded by a fluid-filled membranous sac that cushions and protects him or her. This fluid is mostly water. Prior to labor, the membranes rupture, and this fluid leaks or gushes out, being expelled from the body. This is why it's called the water breaking. Labor should start spontaneously within twelve to twenty-four hours. There are times when the physician has to break the water to induce labor if it's not happening when it should.

John 3 says Jesus told Nicodemus that he must be born again, but he wondered how he would reenter his mother's womb or uterus. Jesus essentially told him that we must be born of water and the Spirit. Also, in John 7, He spoke of "rivers of living water" flowing out of our bellies, while relating this to the Spirit. The water of the Spirit is shown moving throughout scripture. Coming out of Egypt, the children of Israel had to pass through the waters to be birthed into the Promised Land. The waters had to "break" apart for Moses to "deliver" them. In Ezekiel 47, we see the waters gushing or breaking from the temple, flowing all the way down to the Dead Sea and bringing life to everything it touches. This is witnessed in Isaiah 35, when it says the waters would "break out" in the wilderness, bringing life to the desert. Also, Revelation 22 lets us know that Christ is the temple and the door from which these waters flow.

Zechariah 14:8 foretells how these waters would flow from Jerusalem through Christ to the apostles and then to the whole world with the gospel. Luke 24 and Acts 1 said He would give them the power of the Holy Spirit to be witnesses, starting at Jerusalem. Matthew 13:47 speaks of the kingdom of heaven being like a net gathering all kinds of fish, which represents souls being pulled in.

Everything points to the water breaking as the moving of the Spirit of God in order to birth souls and ministries into His kingdom. It means that it's close to happening for you when God moves by His power. It is also letting us know that this is part of the labor process, and we must allow it to flow through us. Or we must discern in which direction it's flowing and go with it in order to be effective spiritually. It won't be by human power or effort but by the strength and wisdom of the Spirit that we succeed in birthing and performing our ministries (Zech. 4:6).

Another thought comes from John 19:34, when the soldier pierced Jesus in the side, resulting in "blood and water" coming out. This, in combination with 1 John 5:8, lets us see that the breaking of the water and the blood at Calvary plays not only a vital role in our personal justification and sanctification but also in any ministry that we birth or partake. Even though we can appear successful, any efforts outside of Christ will be a vain effort.

5. *Sudden burst of energy.* Some women report a sudden burst of energy. It may occur twenty-four to forty-eight hours before the onset of labor. Women must be careful at this point because they may overexert themselves and be excessively tired when the actual labor begins. The cause of this energy burst is unknown.

Before your spiritual labor begins, you may experience a burst of energy to do a whole lot of things for God while helping other people or preparing for the birth of your ministry. You may have the energy to go to every ministry function in and out of town in hope of gaining a network of people to be there for you when your "grand day" occurs. You have to be careful not to expend too much energy so that you are not worn out when the actual time comes to birth it. At this time, you may want to please everyone and have everything together, but it's not possible. Sometimes you have to slow down and take fewer engagements so that you'll have adequate push and energy to bring your ministry to pass. Virtue always will go out of you when you're doing ministry, so don't burn out; take time to refuel.

During true labor, the contractions produce progressive dilatation of the cervix. Keep this in mind while birthing your ministry. The frequent pains and discomforts actually push the door open to give birth to your vision. Sometimes you may have an increase in pain, stress, and pressure on your job. It may push the door open to birth a vision that you've been carrying for a long time. If it's false labor, no door will open for you to leave or start your own business.

Stages of Labor

Labor is categorized into three major stages (some practitioners add a fourth stage). The first stage is when true labor begins and ends when the cervix is completely dilated. This stage is further divided into the latent, active, and transition phases.

During the latent, or early, phase, contractions get regular and increase in frequency, duration, and intensity. This phase lasts longer if it's a woman's first pregnancy. When the pain and discomfort lasts longer than in the past, it may be that her time has come. If it's your first experience, expect it to take a little longer than for someone who's done it multiple times. Don't get discouraged by comparing yourself to someone who's given birth to several ministries. They should be making things happen in a shorter period of time because of their experience.

There's a lot of excitement during this phase because the woman is finally relieved that true labor has started. She has increased discomfort as well as anxiety, but she can cope with it because her time is drawing near. Some women are very talkative and willing to answer questions concerning themselves or their pregnancies.

The same is going on with your vision or ministry that's about to be birthed. You're excited and can deal with the discomforts at this point because you understand what they mean. You're very excited at this time concerning what's about to manifest in your life. You love talking about what God has given you and what is about to happen. I've experienced this personally while writing this final chapter in the book. I'm more excited than ever and talk about it more, even though the pains are here.

The active phase is when the baby is moving down and the cervix is starting to dilate. This is the time for the woman to move to where she's going to deliver. It's also the time for her to practice breathing techniques. When used correctly, these techniques can cause a woman to become more relaxed and able to cope with the pain of labor. The panting technique is supposed to lift the abdominal wall off the contracting uterus to help decrease the pain. As you go through this phase of increased pain and progress toward delivery, the breathing is suggestive of reliance on the Spirit of God to lift the burden of the ministry. With your pattern-paced breathing, relax and allow the Holy Spirit to be the wind that causes you to soar into your destiny. Don't stress yourself out. God is going to bring it to pass.

The end of the first stage of labor is called the transition phase. There may be feelings of helplessness, anger, and fear. The pressure may be so great that she feels she can't take it anymore, or she just wants to be done with it. She may be very restless, irritable, or even have difficulty understanding directions. Don't be surprised if the woman is withdrawn and doesn't want anyone to say anything to her. This is the most difficult and challenging phase, but it's also the shortest of the three.

You're now experiencing more pain, and it's lasting longer than you've ever had to endure in your spiritual pregnancy. You can experience all kinds of emotions during this phase, but it's going to be over very soon. While writing this chapter, I experienced pain and anger that I could not shake. Ordinarily, I could get over this type of experience rather easily, but this time, the pain wouldn't go away. Then it dawned on me: I was in true labor, and this book was about to be birthed. God allowed me to experience this discomfort near the end of this last chapter so that I could more effectively convey this message to you.

Over the years, I've birthed different visions, ministries, and even music projects. I remember experiencing severe pain and pressure with each one. At the time, I was irritable and angry at what was happening to me. But now I see that it was a part of the process of my pregnancy, being in the transition phase, for I was about to deliver something great.

The second stage begins with the cervix fully dilated and ends with the delivery of the baby. Through much pain, stress, and discomfort, the door to birth your dream or ministry is now wide open. You've changed positions, trying to get comfortable, but the baby is dictating things now. It's coming forth, urging you to "push" and saying, "Ready or not, here I come." Therefore, it's time to move into whatever position you need. Second Chronicles 20 instructed the people of God to get into position for what He was about to do through them. An awesome "delivery" took place. Your ministry, vision, or idea has now been birthed. It's alive!

The third and final stage is when the placental separation and delivery take place. The blood rushes out to complete the process. Bleeding causes the formation of a hematoma, which is a large collection of blood that pools in the uterus. It accelerates the process of the separation of the placenta so that it can be expelled. In other words, the blood of Christ causes the completion of the delivery or birth of your ministry. It starts with the blood (the missed period) and ends with the blood. Therefore, never, ever leave the blood out of what you're doing for God.

There's no end to the things that can be discussed concerning "spiritual pregnancy." There are numerous examples in the Old Testament, where children are born and given names based on the current situation. You may not understand the magnitude of what you're carrying until after it's birthed. Even though it has to develop, there should be some characteristics of you as well as God—if, indeed, He fathered it.

Sometimes a woman is pregnant, carrying multiple babies at the same time. If you are passionate about several things simultaneously and have ideas or a vision for them, you deliver them all at the same time. It may be as it was with Rebekah in Genesis 25, when she was having difficulty with her pregnancy. She was barren, but God had blessed her to become pregnant. She began to seek God as to why she was having such difficulty if it was truly a blessing from Him. He told her it was because she was carrying "two nations" in her womb. Sometimes you're carrying twins, triplets, or even more to reach nations of people. This may be the reason for your inner turmoil. Maybe, you're carrying a diverse, multifaceted, or multicultural ministry to reach a large number of people. Perhaps you have a local ministry within your church or in your community. Whether it's regional, statewide, or global, remember that if you're given much, much will be required of you. Usually, if a woman delivers multiple children, family members and other people get involved with the care of those infants. You may be the one who delivers several children at one time, but God will have people there to assist you. Just make sure you get good prenatal care from your spiritual obstetrician. Get your team together before your actual due date and get ready to labor.

Spiritual Transplant Rejection

Before concluding, I would like to briefly mention one last condition that fascinates me: transplant rejection. Whenever you get a blood transfusion or organ transplant, there's always the possibility that the body's immune system will react adversely to defend itself against the foreign substance. In the case of a transplanted organ (if it's not from an identical twin), there is always a risk of the body attacking and destroying the new tissue. There has to be as close a match as possible to avoid rejection. The blood type and tissue type are tested and cross-matched for compatibility. (Thank God for the "cross" match that was performed at Calvary by Christ, my Savior, before performing a heart transplant on me.) A perfectly good kidney and a good candidate can end up destroying each other if they aren't compatible. Although no two people are just alike, they must be tested for suitability before a transplant to avoid the serious danger of rejection. Even if they are compatible, the person usually has to be on immunosuppressive therapy and stay on anti-rejection medicine the rest of his or her life. Rejection can be hyperacute, acute, or chronic. The reaction can manifest symptoms within minutes or gradually over several months.

Application

If you were not born into a church, ministry, or organization but later were transplanted, you may experience rejection. You may wonder why there's so much resistance or hostility toward you when you go to certain churches or ministries—it could be spiritual transplant rejection. You may not fit into that particular ministry or organization. If you don't see eye to eye or never really catch the vision of a ministry, there's always the risk of rejection. Some professional football coaches like to draft players who fit their system and train them accordingly. When a player is drafted and trained by one coach and later gets traded to another team with an entirely different system, he may not fit. It could be a highly talented and knowledgeable player who gets rejected simply because his programming is just too different. Football or basketball teams and even churches may have a highly talented person that they try to build around but never really become successful. Sometimes they may win a championship but never build the dynasty they could have had, unless they get rid of that highly talented yet destructive person.

On the other hand, people or an organization can reject you because of intimidation or just plain resistance to change. It's good to understand that you don't have to do anything wrong to get rejected. It could be as it was when Saul rejected David because Saul had been rejected by God (1 Sam. 15:23–28, 18:12). Sometimes people fight you in a ministry just because they see what God has put on your life. Instead of seeing you as another vital part of the whole, they are threatened by your gift or anointing. They may need you as a kidney or liver transplant, but to their own detriment, they fight to the death of their own ministry. This is why Paul said there shouldn't be any division within the church body (1 Cor. 12). We must always be aware that rejection can occur almost immediately or several months later. One of the main reasons rejection occurs is that people stop taking their anti-rejection medication. Sometimes you see right away that a newly transplanted person is not going to work out. At other times, you think people are with you for the long run but later the symptoms start manifesting. There's inflammation, irritability, chronic complaining, or simply a poor working relationship. As believers, we must love our neighbors as we love ourselves and accept people's differences (Rom. 14–15). The Word of God has plenty of anti-rejection medication in the scriptures. But it's so vital to find as close a match as possible before joining a different church or new ministry. You don't want to cause an unnecessary hypersensitivity reaction because you failed to check for compatibility. It's sad to always have to suppress the gifts and abilities you've been blessed with because where you are is not suitable or a close enough match to operate freely, whether in music, teaching, singing, preaching, and so on.

We must always look to our ultimate example—Christ. He came to His own people and was rejected (Isa. 53:3; John 1:11). The cross that He bore was the epitome of rejection. He actually donated His whole body to us. The scriptures say that we have received His mind (1 Cor. 2:16). Researchers have been working on ways to desensitize people by filtering out antibodies so they can better receive certain transplants that may not be compatible. Spiritually, we must regularly renew our minds in order to always be in good standing with Christ. Since He donated His body to us, He asks us to donate or present our bodies to Him as living sacrifices (Rom. 12:1–2). Strive to be more God-conscious than self-conscious. There's no reason we can't work together if we are the body of Christ collectively. He gave us His blood and all His organs. We now have His blood type and His DNA. This makes us all the perfect match in Christ. Stay on your anti-rejection medication, always praying, "Not my will, but thine, be done," (Luke 22:42), and accept that people are different and have different gifts from yours. I need you, and you need me. Together, we make each other complete.

To Be Continued

As you traveled with me on this journey through the human body, you learned how God speaks to us through numerous disorders and conditions. I trust that you're starting to recognize and diagnose spiritual conditions and will get better as you continue to pray and engage in your own personal studies. As long as there are countless diseases and new ones being discovered regularly, there always will be new spiritual messages to learn and apply.

By no stretch of the imagination am I a Bible scholar, physician, or scientist. Nevertheless, to be entrusted with discovering and sharing practical spiritual truths from our physical bodies is quite the privilege. Jesus often taught publicly using parables while privately explaining the meanings to His disciples. He would let them know He wanted them to understand certain "mysteries" concerning the kingdom of heaven (Matt. 13:11). If you've studied the Bible for any length of time, you may have come across a few mysterious passages. The keys to accessing this wealth of insight are spiritual intimacy, hunger, and study. Studying the human body can be as challenging and perplexing as the spiritual things of scripture. If you're up to the task, it will enhance your faith and deeply enrich your spiritual walk.

I believe God has intertwined the physical and spiritual body in such a way to reveal a mystery here that unlocks powerful insight into the workings of both. The more we search to understand the functioning of the human body, the more we can understand how things work spiritually. And the more we study scripture and the spiritual body, the greater potential we have for understanding the health of the physical body. Whether you're in ministry or simply a believer, you will never be without fresh information to share.

RESOURCES

1. "About Cancer, Diagnosis and Staging." National Cancer Institute. March 2015. Accessed June 10, 2015. http://www.cancer.gov/about-cancer/diagnosis-staging/symptoms.
2. "About HIV/AIDS." Centers for Disease Control and Prevention. Accessed October 20, 2015. http://www.cdc.gov/hiv/basics/whatishiv.html.
3. "A Brief Overview of the 2007 National Diabetes Fact Sheet." The Frannie Foundation. Accessed June 10, 2015. http://thefranniefoundation.org/news-research/brief-overview-of-the-2007-national-diabetes-fact-sheet/.
4. American Heart Association News. "U.S. Death Rate Rises Slightly in 2015, as Heart Disease Deaths Level Off." Accessed November 16, 2015. http://news.heart.org/u-s-death-rate-rises-slightly-in-2015-as-heart-disease-deaths-level-off/.
5. "Cancer." The Mayo Clinic Staff, Diseases and Conditions. Accessed January 11, 2016. http://www.mayoclinic.org/diseases-conditions/cancer/basics/symptoms/con-20032378.
6. "Dehydration." The Mayo Clinic Staff, Diseases and Conditions. Accessed January 11, 2016. http://www.mayoclinic.org/diseases-conditions/dehydration/basics/definition/con-20030056>.

7. "Diabetic Hypoglycemia." The Mayo Clinic Staff, Diseases and Conditions. Accessed January 11, 2016. http://www.mayoclinic.org/diseases-conditions/diabetes/basics/definition/con-20033091>.
8. "Immune System." Kids Health from Nemours Foundation. May 2015. Accessed March 14, 2016. http://kidshealth.org/en/parents/immune.html#kha_11.
9. "Infertility." Centers for Disease Control. Accessed May 11, 2015. http://www.cdc.gov/reproductivehealth/Infertility/.
10. Lobo, V., A. Patil, A. Phatak, and N. Chandra. "Free Radicals, Antioxidants and Functional Foods: Impact on Human Health." Pharmacognosy Review. July–Dec. 2010. Accessed November 1, 2015. http://www.ncbi.nlm.nih.gov/pmc/articles/PMC3249911/.
11. "More on How HIV Causes AIDS." National Institute of Allergy and Infectious Diseases. January 5, 2009. Accessed October 30, 2015. https://www.niaid.nih.gov/topics/HIVAIDS/Understanding/howHIVCausesAIDS/Pages/howhiv.aspx.
12. Olds, Sally B., Marcia L. London, and Patricia W. Ladewig. *Maternal-Newborn Nursing / A Family-Centered Approach*. 5th ed. Menlo Park, CA: Addison-Wesley Nursing, 1996.
13. "Safety and Prevention." Rape, Abuse, and Incest National Network (RAINN). Accessed March 2016. https://www.rainn.org/safety-prevention.
14. "Sexual Assault and STDs." Centers for Disease Control and Prevention. Accessed May 12, 2015. http://www.cdc.gov/std/treatment/2010/sexual-assault.htm.
15. "Signs and Symptoms of Cancer." American Cancer Society. August 11, 2014. Accessed November 11,

2015. http://www.cancer.org/cancer/cancerbasics/signs-and-symptoms-of-cancer.

16. "Systemic Lupus Erythematosus." Johns Hopkins Medicine. Accessed November 24, 2015. http://www.hopkinsmedicine.org/healthlibrary/conditions/arthritis_and_other_rheumatic_diseases/systemic_lupus_erythematosus_lupus_85,P00058/.

17. "The Salty Stuff." National Institutes of Health. March 2010. Accessed March 1, 2016. https://newsinhealth.nih.gov/2010/march/feature1.htm.

18. Thibodeau, Gary A., and Kevin T. Patton. *Structure & Function of the Body.* 13th ed. Saint Louis, MO: Mosby/Elsevier, 2008.

19. "Transplant Rejection: Hyperacute, Acute, Chronic & Graft Versus Host." Stomp on Step 1. May 15, 2016. http://www.stomponstep1.com/transplant-rejection-hyperacute-acute-chronic-graft-versus-host/.

20. "What are the Organs of the Immune System." PubMed. January 14, 2013. Accessed March 15, 2016. http://www.ncbi.nlm.nih.gov/pubmedhealth/PMH0072579/.

CPSIA information can be obtained
at www.ICGtesting.com
Printed in the USA
BVOW04s1121040517
482982BV00017B/3/P